In Praise of Forgetting

Also by David Rieff

In Praise of Forgetting

Historical Memory and Its Ironies

DAVID RIEFF

Yale UNIVERSITY PRESS

New Haven and London

Published with assistance from the foundation established in memory of Amasa Stone Mather of the Class of 1907, Yale College.

Yale University Press books may be purchased in quantity for educational, business, or promotional use. For information, please e-mail sales.press@yale.edu (U.S. office) or sales@yaleup.co.uk (U.K. office).

Set in Minion type by IDS Infotech, Ltd.
Printed in the United States of America.

Library of Congress Control Number: 2015954282
ISBN 978-0-300-18279-8 (cloth : alk. paper)

A catalogue record for this book is available from the British Library.

This paper meets the requirements of ANSI/NISO Z39.48–1992 (Permanence of Paper).

10 9 8 7 6 5 4 3 2 1

This book is for Dasantha Pillay.

Too long a sacrifice can make a stone of the heart.

—W. B. YEATS

Contents

Acknowledgments

Throughout its gestation, this book has had more and better friends already than any writer could sensibly hope for. It also has a slightly checkered history. In 2009, Louise Adler and Elise Berg at the University of Melbourne Press were kind enough to invite me to write a polemic on political memory, which they published two years later under the title *Against Remembrance*. *In Praise of Forgetting* builds on the work I did then, and so I want to thank Louise, Elise, and their colleagues "in the name" of both books.

In recent years, I have begun spending as much time as I can manage in Ireland. But being a Hibernophile hardly qualifies me as an expert in Irish history and politics, and on those questions I have had the good fortune to have been the beneficiary of the learning and insight of Rosemary Byrne, Kevin O'Rourke, Cormac Ó Gráda, Tom Arnold, Paul Durcan, Denis Staunton, and John Banville in Dublin, and Jim Fahy in Galway. They are of course in no way, shape, or form responsible for the uses to which I have put that learning.

The same disclaimers apply to the "tutorial" on Jewish history, including on Yosef Yerushalmi's work, that my old and true friend Leon Wieseltier has been trying, with what I suspect he would say has been mixed success, to give me for decades now. They also apply to two newer friends, R. R. Reno in New York and Fr. Bernard Treacy in Dublin, who, though their views seem to me to diverge on a number of important issues of interpretation, have both taught me much about the Catholic understanding of the relationship between history and memory. They will be the best judges of the extent to which I have understood them properly, and, to reiterate, any errors I have made are mine alone.

Since the days when I was his student at Amherst College in what now seems almost like another geological era, and *was* almost forty-five years ago, I have benefited from the learning and friendship of Norman Birnbaum. If I have gotten Löwith, Halbwachs, Renan, and other thinkers on whom I have relied in this book even partly right, this is as much Norman's doing as mine, even if, all these years later, Tönnies still defeats me.

And I would have been defeated in the writing of this book without the extraordinary help I have received during the period in which I was researching it from Megan Campisi, and, during the fact checking after it was finished, from Megan and from Elisa Matula.

Finally, I owe the fact that *In Praise of Forgetting* exists at all to Steve Wasserman, my editor at Yale University Press, whose gift to me it was to make it possible for me to have another bite at the apple of memory and forgetting. Steve and I have known each other practically our entire adult lives. We were young together, middle-aged together, and now we are growing old together. Given that there is no cure for *that*, I can't think of a better friend with whom to have shared and still be sharing the ride.

In Praise of
Forgetting

ONE

Footprints in the Sands of Time, and All That

L awrence Binyon's poem "For the Fallen" was first published in the *London Times* on September 21, 1914, six weeks after the Great War had begun. It is sometimes suggested that Binyon, who was a distinguished art historian as well as a poet (he was the British Museum's Keeper of Oriental Prints and Drawings when the war began), wrote the poem in despair over how many had already died and how many more were being condemned to the same fate. But there is no basis for such a reading. Binyon simply could not have known this, if for no other reason than that it was not till the end of the First Battle of Ypres two months later, an engagement at which the majority of Britain's prewar professional army was either killed or wounded, that people at home began to realize just how terrible a toll the war promised to exact.

In reality, "For the Fallen" is a classic patriotic poem, far closer in spirit to Horace's "Dulce et decorum est pro patria mori" (It is sweet and fitting to die for one's country)—an injunction that actually had been graven into the wall of the chapel of the Royal Military Academy at Sandhurst in 1913—than to the work of the great British soldier-poets such as Wilfred Owen, who would appropriate the motto for one of his finest poems, but only in order to call it "the old lie."

That such prescience regarding what was to come was unavailable to Binyon weeks into the war hardly dishonors him. Too old to serve in the trenches, in 1916 he nonetheless would volunteer for duty as a hospital orderly on the Western Front—no mean commitment. And Binyon's poem has endured. As I write this, 101 years after the First Battle of Ypres, "For the Fallen" remains the quasi-official poem of remembrance, without which virtually no memorial ceremony for the dead of both World War I and World War II in Britain, Canada, Australia, or New Zealand is considered complete. Its fourth and best-known stanza reads:

> They shall grow not old, as we that are left grow old:
> Age shall not weary them, nor the years condemn.
> At the going down of the sun and in the morning
> We will remember them.

In Australia, where the memory of Australians' sacrifice during the First World War, above all during the Dardanelles campaign against the Turks in 1915, played an extraordinarily important role in the forging of the modern Australian state,[1]

1. By the 1920s, Anzac Day, which was first celebrated in both Australia and New Zealand on April 25, 1916, to commemorate the first anniversary of the landing on the Gallipoli peninsula that marked the beginning of that ill-fated campaign, had eclipsed Empire Day, which was held every May 24, Queen Victoria's birthday.

"For the Fallen" is now known as "The Ode of Remembrance." And at many Anzac Day ceremonies, after the fourth stanza is declaimed, it is customary for those present to respond with the words "Lest we forget," as if to the invocation at a church service, which in a sense, of course, it is. In doing so, the participants meld the Binyon poem with Rudyard Kipling's far greater poem "Recessional," from which the line "Lest we forget" is taken, a line that, twice repeated, concludes each of its stanzas, as in this, the best known of them:

> Far-called, our navies melt away;
> On dune and headland sinks the fire:
> Lo, all our pomp of yesterday
> Is one with Nineveh and Tyre!
> Judge of the Nations, spare us yet,
> Lest we forget—lest we forget!

As is so often the case in his work, Kipling had a far more complicated and pessimistic view of the world, above all of the fate of nations, than the memory of him either among his critics or his (sadly diminished number of) admirers would lead one to believe. Although advanced in inverted terms, since the poet is in effect appealing for divine intercession for a deferral of what he knows to be the foreordained outcome, "Lest we forget" is a mournful acknowledgment that such forgetting is inevitable—both on our own parts as individuals and with regard to us after we are gone. Implicit in Kipling's line is a far more terrifying one: "When we forget." In this, "Recessional" echoes the chilling words of Ecclesiastes 1:11: "There is no remembrance of former things; neither shall there be any remembrance of later things that are to come with those that shall come after." And more proximately, Kipling's poem is a gloss—explicitly so, at one point—on Shelley's "Ozymandias" and its unflinching meditation on the ephemeral nature of even the most monumental creations and martial accomplishments of human beings and the societies to which they have belonged.

Deep down, we all know this to be true, however difficult it is to imagine how we could live our daily lives with even a bare minimum of serenity or success without at least acting as if we believed otherwise. For to fully make Ecclesiastes 1:11 our true north would be to live as if we were already dead. And this, a few saints and mystics excepted, and surely their capacities in this regard are inseparable from their disengagement from the world, we cannot do—"No man can stare for long at death or the sun," as La Rochefoucauld said—nor, even were it possible, is there any moral or ethical imperative for our doing so. It is probably true that were we to imagine those of our loved ones whom we will survive only as dust, we might be more loving, more forgiving, more willing to put their wishes and desires before our own. But to do this, we would have to be able to live our lives as if we had already experienced the whole of them, which is a contradiction in terms. For as Kierkegaard said, "Life must be lived forward, but can only be understood backward."

A successful society based on such a focus is still harder to imagine. For while such a society might be more "truthful" in some absolute sense, fostering or conserving a moral conscience within it would be impossible. Even to care about the present would be challenge enough, let alone finding a way to care about either the past or the future. It may be that "the ultimate truth is fearless," as the Buddhist sage Trungpa Rinpoche once put it. But in thinking about history, this particular truth is far more likely to terrify and paralyze than encourage and inspire. As the German philosopher Karl Löwith put it in his now largely forgotten masterpiece *The Meaning of History* (1947), "To ask earnestly the question of the ultimate meaning of history takes one's breath away. It transports us into a vacuum which only hope and faith can fill."

But if we have no other practical choice than to try to live our lives and contribute to our societies as if Ecclesiastes were wrong, this should not manumit us from mustering the courage, at least from time to time, to contemplate the ultimate meaninglessness of history, and to recognize that, to paraphrase Trotsky's quip about war, "You may not be interested in the geological record, but the geological record is interested in you." And even if we radically narrow the frame, excluding not only evolutionary or geological time but also the approximately 192,000 years that elapsed between the emergence in Africa 200,000 years ago of anatomically modern *Homo sapiens* and the advent of proto-writing (usually ideograms) in the sixth millennium before the Common Era—if not, far more pertinently, the emergence of writing and thus of recorded history 2,000 years later in the fourth millennium BCE—there still can be no reprieve from the reality that sooner or later every human accomplishment, like every human being, will be forgotten. It is this that Kipling is inviting his readers to recognize in "Recessional": sooner or later our own polities will vanish just as surely as did Nineveh and Tyre.

What possible historical basis could there be for thinking otherwise? The world of states we live in today has existed for only a comparatively small fraction of recorded history, and a great deal even of that history has already been forgotten by everyone except historians. This applies not only to states with very long histories but even to those with very short ones, of which there are in fact a great many. Italy and Germany in the form they exist today date back only to the nineteenth century, while many of the independent African states that emerged out of the ruins of empire in the mid-twentieth century did so with borders that more often than not were the product of British and French colonial mapmakers and bore little resemblance to the polities that existed before the European imperial conquest of the continent. The modern United States from its beginnings as a collection of colonies to the present day is a little more than four hundred years old. The First Fleet sailed into Botany Bay at the beginning of 1788, which means that the modern Australia has existed for a little more than half that time. Even France, which has been a state in the modern sense for far longer than any other in Europe, can be said to have coalesced into the form it takes today only about six hundred years ago at the earliest. And as Theodore Zeldin has shown in his magisterial *History of France, 1848–1945,* the sense of collective French national identity began as a self-conception largely restricted to the ruling classes and became widely shared by the population as a whole only at the time of the French Revolution; it was not wholly generalized until well into the nineteenth century.

Given how much older China and India are as continuous civilizations, the picture is somewhat different in Asia. But we still cannot speak of a unified Indian state until the advent of the Mughal Empire in the sixteenth century. And even China, by far the oldest state in world history, did not become a unified country until the beginning of the Qin dynasty in the last part of the third century before the Common Era. Again, this may be a very long time in historical terms, but in terms of geological time it is little more than the blink of an eye. We may choose to ignore this, and consider the question exclusively in the context of historical time. Even so, on what basis other than the narcissism of the living or a reckless disregard for history and logic could anyone seriously suggest that even the most coherent and solid of the states that now exist will still be around in anything like the same form in another thousand years, or two, or three?

The reality is that no intelligent person believes anything of the sort. Whereas a believer in one of the great religions might insist that Christianity, Islam, Judaism, and Hinduism are true, and therefore cannot be "forgotten" in the conventional sense of the term (or, at least, can always be "retrieved"),[2] in the secular world, in the deepest sense, it is inconceivable that the political order that characterizes our own era—which, notwithstanding globalization, is still, broadly speaking, one of nation-states—could be immortal, however long-lived it may prove to be. This is not simply a matter of elementary reasoning. For what history actually shows is that throughout all of recorded history, every society without a single exception has proven to be every bit as mortal as individual human beings. To try to think otherwise is a fool's errand. Buddhism, whether it is a religion or not in the conventional sense, is almost certainly the only philosophical system that teaches its adherents that clinging to the past, like clinging to the self, is a forlorn illusion.

This is not to deny that there are good and sufficient reasons for living inside such a consoling conceit. Buddhism promises liberation, but the release from suffering it offers requires a degree of self-abnegation that few modern people have the fortitude to contemplate, let alone successfully practice. So, with apologies to Freud, the illusion that nothing that really matters to we who live now will ever be forgotten by our

---

2. Buddhism is a special case to the degree that it insists on the impermanence of all things, another way of saying it insists that nothing lasts, in the memory or anywhere else.

posterity through the millennia does indeed have a future. For if, despite the consoling fictions offered up by a Kantian perspective that illusion, identified as such or not, today dominates the moral imagination of so many of the most scrupulous and ethically conscientious among us, truth and morality can at times be incommensurable, then the same can and must be said about reality and necessity. As the moral philosopher Bernard Williams once quipped, "The will is as free as it needs to be." Reality may demand that we acknowledge the certainty that all nations and civilizations will eventually vanish just as surely as they arose. But how to reconcile what reality demands with the fact that for most people to live without remission in its shadow would be paralyzing, a slippery slope from knowledge to impotent despair. As Kipling wrote in his memoir, *Something of Myself*, "Every nation, like every individual, walks in a vain show—else it could not live with itself." Instead, as he put it in his poem "Cities and Thrones and Powers," a work every bit as despairing as "Recessional":

> This season's Daffodil,
> She never hears,
> What change, what chance, what chill,
> Cut down last year's;
> But with bold countenance,
> And knowledge small,
> Esteems her seven days' continuance
> To be perpetual.

Perhaps it is consolation enough if we can believe, even while acknowledging that history has no intrinsic meaning, that it still possesses another kind of meaning, one derived from the way human beings order their experience of it and their aspirations for how it might be better ordered in the present and in the future, thus infusing it with significance and, of course, passing it along to their posterity. But how to reconcile ourselves to the reality that even such constructed meanings are mortal, and take on board the fact that sooner or later the past will recede in importance before it is lost entirely? For here the personal oblivion we call death and the societal oblivion we call forgetting are two sides of the same coin.

"Birth was the death of him," wrote Beckett, and it's as applicable to civilizations as it is to individuals. But just as it is possible for at least some people to shift the center of their perceptions from their own personal fate—nonbeing—to an other-centered focus (and this is probably the only way those of us who find the prospect of our own extinction unbearable can keep from being driven mad by the knowledge of it), there is no reason why the same shifting should not be possible with respect to our collective fate. And if this is even partly right, then the mortality of societies and civilizations need not be regarded solely as a calamity. For a world in which everything endured through all eternity in a form recognizable to those of us living now all the way to the end of humanity's lifespan as a species is as unimaginable as the fantasy of personal immortality, which also posits such an outcome.

And might not a Freudian detect an essential connection between the brute facts of our personal and collective transience, our ephemerality (in its denotative meaning of "lasting for a markedly brief time"), and the need to see in human life a level of meaning that an individual endowed with absolute rationality would see through in an instant, discerning instead our inevitable biological fate? Freud understood that too much rationality so gravely undermines group life that past a certain threshold no society can survive it. And regardless of whether we completely accept Freud's generalization, we hardly need a profound insight into human nature to understand that to remain productive—and possibly even to stay entirely sane—we human beings need to behave *as if* the era in which we are fated to live and die and, after we have been extinguished forever, a relatively short period of the future to come about whose essential characteristics we feel that the present allows us to foresee would be recognizable to us were we to be resurrected at some more far-off point in the future.

Most science-fiction writing and television- and moviemaking incarnates this conceit. For although their stories are usually set in the future, far more often than not they are actually transpositions of events taking place today that reflect the hopes and fears of the present age. Sometimes, in what might be called the hopeful, *Star Trek* model, they extrapolate from our accomplishments and our desires; at other times—the *Planet of the Apes* model—they mirror our follies and our fears. The Los Angeles of *Blade Runner*, to cite an example of the second type, is far more reflective of a late-twentieth-century white American's dystopic view of the world that exists today, one increasingly made up of people of color, than it is an imagining of the future.

Certainly, few novelists or scriptwriters working in the genre have conceived of their project in the way that the British science-fiction writer Olaf Stapledon did when he wrote that his work demanded "a detachment from all private, all social, all racial ends" and contained within it "a kind of piety toward fate." And in his novels *Last and First Men: A Story of the Near and Far Future* (1930) and its sequel, *Star Maker* (1937), Stapledon indeed tried to encompass nothing less than the evolution of the human species—"this brief music that is man," as he described it at the conclusion of the first book—from the twentieth century to two billion years into the future.

But Stapledon is an outlier. As a general rule, even in science fiction the historical reach of the imagination, whether backward or forward, is limited. And if imaginative literature has a shelf life, so too does historical memory. Take Australia and New Zealand, the two countries where Binyon's poem remains most resonant. As I write this in 2015, the Remembrance Day ceremonies that have been held since the end of World War I almost certainly make not just historical but ethical sense to a majority of the citizens of both countries. In doing so, they are trying to ensure that those whose ancestors fought in that war continue to be honored, while the recent immigrants to Australia and New Zealand, most of them non-European, who make up an increasing proportion of the citizens of both nations, are, depending on one's political views, invited or pressured to assimilate themselves into the national sense of belonging that these ceremonies serve to instill and subsequently to confirm.

In other countries, though, analogous celebrations of national sacrifice have fallen into desuetude. Anyone who has driven through the small towns of Massachusetts, Connecticut, or Pennsylvania that were founded before the American Civil War will have seen the monuments to the local men who lost their lives serving in the Union Army, while monuments to the Confederate war dead are all but ubiquitous in towns of similar longevity throughout the South. Between the end of the war in 1865 and the centennial of its beginning in 1961, such historical landmarks served as the focal points of widespread remembrance ceremonies. As with every project focused on historical remembrance, whether the goal in any given instance is to forge it, sustain or affirm it, challenge it, reconstruct it, or replace it, there was nothing innocent about these commemorations. As Caroline E. Janney puts it in her remarkable *Remembering the Civil War: Reunion and the Limits of Reconciliation,* "As early as 1865, the veterans and civilians who survived the four bloody years of war were acutely aware that people were actively shaping what should be remembered—and omitted—from the historical record. . . . What individuals and communities elected to tell of the war held enormous potential for staking claims of authority and power."

Annual observances honoring the dead were initiated by Confederate war veterans in 1866. Two years later, in 1868, the Union veterans organization, the Grand Army of the Republic, followed suit. On both sides, women played a key role. In contemporary France, the debate over how the country's colonial past should be commemorated is often referred to as the "memory wars." A strong argument can be made that in the French context the expression is excessive. But there can be no doubt that between the end of the American Civil War and the end of the nineteenth century, the metaphor was an entirely appropriate way of describing the incompatible, and on both sides immensely bitter, accounts northerners and (white) southerners put forward as to why the war had been fought. Given the fact that the South had been defeated, it is more than a little surprising that these "dueling" memories could be maintained. After all, when a war ends with a crushing victory by one side, as that one certainly did, the victory confers the power unilaterally to shape the collective memory of the conflict—a power that the victors nearly always exercise, as the American, British, French, and Russian occupiers did in post–World War II Germany and the Tutsi-led Rwandan Patriotic Front did in post-genocide Rwanda. Historically, it is only when there is no clear winner that both sides may be able to sustain their own incompatible memories. An example of this is the

Bosnia-Herzegovina that came into being after the Dayton Peace Agreement of 1995 brought the war to an end.

It is for this reason that many historians of the Civil War and of Reconstruction have argued that, as Janney summarizes it, "White northerners eventually capitulated to Confederate memory." Given that from the end of Reconstruction in the 1870s white northerners clearly capitulated to southern segregationism, this would seem beyond debate. And while Janney is adamant that at least for the late nineteenth century the historians' claim is too broad, she readily concedes that it did become the case in the twentieth century. By the 1930s, she writes, white Americans had become "increasingly receptive to the Lost [i.e., Confederate] Cause." She points to the emblematic case of the extraordinary commercial success of the film *Gone with the Wind,* noting that "Americans could not get enough of the romantic epic depicting white southern resolve in the face of defeat."

But even assuming Janney is correct about the timing, what was quickly forgotten by virtually every white American, northerner and southerner alike, was that the first celebration of what eventually would become the national holiday first known as Decoration Day and now called Memorial Day took place on May 1, 1865, and was organized by African American freedmen in Charleston, South Carolina, in honor of the 257 Union soldiers who had died in captivity in the local racecourse that the Confederates had used as a prison camp during the war, and whom the freedmen had earlier reburied properly. The event drew more than ten thousand participants (including a brigade of Union soldiers with three African American units, the 54th Massachusetts and the 34th and 104th Colored Troops), as well as drawing wide attention in the national press at the time—a correspondent for the *New York Tribune* wrote that the event was "a procession of mourners and friends [such] as South Carolina and the United States never saw before." But for post-Reconstruction white America, the event might just as well never have taken place. It was only black Americans who, as Janney puts it, "continued to offer up a counter-memory of the Civil War and Reconstruction" completely at odds with what the African American historian Dorothy Sterling despairingly and angrily described in 1961 as a false picture of the conflict, one in which "brave brother [fought] against brother, with both separately but equally righteous in their causes."

In the early twenty-first century, Memorial Day commemorations themselves largely serve as occasions for a generalized, watered-down patriotism from which the Civil War and the reasons it was fought are increasingly excluded, in favor of honoring the dead of all U.S. wars, but also as the occasion for a three-day holiday weekend during which both the most important American automobile race, the Indianapolis 500, and an important golf championship, the Memorial, are held. It is not that the Civil War no longer resonates in the United States. In a country in which the wound of racism has never been fully staunched, that would be impossible. But it is not a Memorial Day now leached of all its historical specificity but rather the Confederate battle flag that still flies in several southern state capitals and is incorporated into several of these states' flags that keeps the memory of the war alive. That they are there at all is the product of a brilliantly executed political campaign largely orchestrated between the end of Reconstruction and 1915 by Confederate veterans' groups, and even more importantly, as Caroline Janney has shown in another fine study, *Burying the Dead but Not the Past: Ladies' Memorial Associations and the Lost Cause,* by organizations of white southern women dedicated, in Janney's words, to "perpetuating nostalgia for the

Confederate past, or for what has come to be known as the Lost Cause."

Civil rights groups have been warning since the 1950s that continuing to fly these flags was not only immoral but dangerous, and called for their removal. Their worst fears were realized when it became clear that the Confederate battle flag had been an inspiration to the white-supremacist terrorist Dylann Roof, who in June 2015 walked into the evening service at the Emanuel African Methodist Episcopal Church in Charleston, one of the oldest AME churches in the United States, and opened fire, killing nine people, including Senator Clementa Pinckney, the senior pastor. In the aftermath of the massacre, even white southerners who had previously defended official displays of the flag were forced to bow to public pressure to put an end to its use, and in the (particularly egregious) case of South Carolina, finally to stop flying it from atop the state capitol.

In the aftermath of Roof's acts, the question of why the Civil War had been fought became, for the first time in decades, part of the mainstream debate.[3] Many whites, northerners and southerners alike, who had seemed impervious to the proposition that the Confederacy was not a noble lost cause and that celebrating the memory of a secession that had taken place in order to preserve slavery was anything but harmless, began to reconsider their views when confronted by the undeniable fact that the racism that had been the Confederacy's raison d'être still lived on in people like Roof. If any good news could be

---

3. So did the issue of the laxity of U.S. gun laws, but even those optimistic about the use of the Confederate flag finally being ended were under no illusions that American gun laws were going to change one iota as a result of the slaughter.

found, it was that, however diminished its importance in the American imagination it may have been 150 years after it had ended, the remembrance of the Civil War remained at least somewhat accessible to many if not perhaps to most Americans.

But imagine as a thought experiment that the focus of Dylann Roof's racist hatred had been Native Americans rather than blacks, and that he had struck at a church on a reservation somewhere in Massachusetts. Even assuming that the shock would have been as great, there could have been no similar reservoir of historical memory to draw upon that, whether accurately or inaccurately (an important question in its own right but not relevant here), could have linked the crimes of the past with the crimes of the present. The reasons for this would have had nothing to do with history and everything to do with what Americans remember and what they have forgotten. Yet so searing and cataclysmic had been King Philip's War of 1675–76, also known as Metacom's Rebellion, that in its immediate aftermath, and for a century thereafter, it would have been inconceivable for either the settlers of the Plymouth Bay Colony or the native Wampanoag and Narragansett nations of Massachusetts and Rhode Island that, in the hoariest trope of the language of remembrance, "anyone would ever forget" it. For in the two years during which it raged, the war almost succeeded in destroying the Plymouth Colony, and at least for a time put an end to the European conquest of the northeastern part of what would become the United States.

On a per capita basis, King Philip's War was the bloodiest in American history. Most of the surviving Native American warriors were executed, and their wives and children transported to the West Indies and sold as slaves. By 1830 the Native American population of Massachusetts and Rhode Island had decreased by about 60–80 percent. Settler losses were far smaller but large enough for two eminent historians of the war to describe it as having posed "a real threat to the colony's continued prosperity, perhaps even to its survival." And yet, professional historians aside, King Philip's War is almost never talked about, even by Americans familiar with the Trail of Tears, President Jackson's ethnic cleansing of the Seminoles, Cherokee, Chickasaw, Choctaw, and Muscogee, and with the genocidal wars the U.S. army conducted against Native American nations of the Great Plains and the Southwest.

What this shows is that the historical importance of an event in its own time and in the decades that follow offers no guarantee that it will be remembered in the next century, let alone for many centuries after. A case can certainly be made that reminding the Americans of today of what happened during King Philip's War might be salutary morally. But even assuming that it would be possible to do this, at some point in history even events as terrible as that conflict will be forgotten, if only, to put it starkly, to make room for the memory of other, less distant events, just as those alive today must sooner or later die to make room for those yet to be born. And whether one regrets this or not, forgetting and being forgotten are what must happen sooner or later. Would even the most historically minded among us claim that there is a civic duty or a moral imperative to hold services of remembrance annually in honor of the Norman and Anglo-Saxon dead of the Battle of Hastings of 1066 or to mourn the sacrifice of those who fell at the Battles of Sekigahara in 1600 and Osaka Castle in 1615 that led to the establishment of the Tokugawa shogunate in Japan?

At least those battles are still recalled, however superficially and sentimentally, by most educated people in Britain and Japan, respectively, although whether there is any practical use in doing so, for non–history buffs and those who live near where these battles took place (where commemorations still generate dependable streams of tourist income), is not as self-evident as the reigning pieties about remembrance seem to insist. In any case, the farther one goes back in time, say to the battles of the Chu-Han War in China (206–202 BCE) or to the Battle of Salamis between the Athenians and the Persians (480 BCE), the more questionable any moral justification for commemorating such events becomes. And yet these battles were as critical in their time, as firmly entrenched in the minds and hearts of those who lived through them and for many generations to come, as defining moments for their civilizations, as the destruction of the World Trade Center on September 11, 2001, is for so many people today, Americans and non-Americans alike.

This does not mean that there is no interest in studying the Battle of Salamis; indeed, one can argue plausibly that, because the second half of the twentieth century and the first two decades of the twenty-first have been something of a golden age for historical scholarship, more is known today about the wars between the Greek city-states and Persia that culminated with the Athenians' victory at Salamis than was understood in Europe during the eighteenth and nineteenth centuries when, culturally, Hellenism provided a central model for poets and philosophers (and to some extent architects) from Schelling and Goethe to Byron and, though to a lesser extent, Matthew Arnold. The German veneration was so extreme that in 1935, the British scholar Eliza Butler could write a book she matter-of-factly and with little fear of contradiction from her peers titled *The Tyranny of Greece over Germany*. The last iteration of this was Heidegger's contention that the only truly philosophical languages were classical Greek and German.

Another version of the eighteenth- and nineteenth-century European elite's obsession with Greece and Rome was its centrality to the self-conception of the British Empire. As David Gilmour put it in his fine study *The Ruling Caste: Imperial Lives in the Victorian Raj,* "British officials [in India] had begun to think of themselves as Romans by the end of the eighteenth century." And as Gilbert Murray, the Regius Professor of Greek at Oxford between 1908 and 1924, wrote, "At home, England is Greek. In the Empire she is Roman," a sentiment that Kipling echoes in a number of his best stories, notably "A Centurion of the Thirtieth," where the Roman officers and legionaries are clearly transpositions of the civil servants and soldiers of his beloved Raj. Even when their empire had ended, many members of the British elite told themselves that the United Kingdom could continue to enact a global role by playing Greece to the American empire's Rome—a fantasy that Christopher Hitchens brilliantly anatomized in his *Blood, Class, and Nostalgia: Anglo-American Ironies.*

This was almost certainly the last contemporary appropriation of classical Greek and Roman history.[4] Though there are other causes, to be sure, the eclipse of Latin and Greek as school subjects in Europe and North America has all but ensured the rupture since one cannot be tyrannized by a past with whose cultural and historical references one is entirely unfamiliar. The Greco-Roman past lasted far longer than did the collective memories of most other historical epochs. But the 2,500 years between the Battle of Salamis and the early twenty-first century have finally put an end to it. We can still admire the *Iliad* and Cicero, the Pantheon and the Acropolis, and be inspired by their force and beauty, but only in a form stripped of any authority

4. The American empire has other myths (above all that it is not an empire); the modern-day Chinese empire will have still others, though as yet these are still largely on the drawing board.

over our moral and political imaginations. As vehicles for our mythmaking about ourselves, they are as good as lost to us.

But what a run! In most cases, the connection to earlier political orders, and to the art and thought they produce, is severed far more quickly. Think of Rubens's portraits of the seventeenth-century English nobility; in their own time, these were clearly understood as glorifications of the Stuart dynasty and as apologias in pictorial form for the divine right of kings. Today, the political and moral beliefs and understandings that are at the heart of Rubens's work, informing his way of seeing, have no hold over us precisely because he was so much a man of his time—indeed, in many ways its biographer. We have only to contrast him with Turner, whom art critic John Berger once described as "a man alone, surrounded by implacable and indifferent forces." Turner is still accessible to us not because he was a better painter than Rubens but rather because, unlike Rubens, he exists outside his own time, thanks to the logic of his work, thus allowing even those who are indifferent to the tradition from which he developed to understand him as their contemporary.

Of course, most painters whose work still matters to us are more in the mold of Rubens than of Turner. And as long as the past remains legible to the present, we may have preferences but we do not have to choose. But what happens when the past, even the quite recent past, becomes illegible? To take another example from the history of painting, Picasso was interested in Velázquez, who died 220 years before he was born. But in the early twenty-first century, young painters are rarely interested even in their predecessors of 50 years before them, let alone those separated by centuries. And once the fundamental disconnection of the processes by which the past of an artistic, or political, or ethical tradition is transmitted down through the generations has been achieved, it is difficult to see how it can ever be successfully undone or redressed. Admittedly, this is not a matter of forgetting in the proper sense of the word: one cannot forget what one never knew. As the philosopher and sociologist Theodor Adorno puts it in *Minima Moralia,* "Just as voluntary memory and utter oblivion always belonged together, organized fame and remembrance lead ineluctably to nothingness."

TWO

Must We Deform the Past in Order to Preserve It?

Everything will indeed be forgotten sooner or later, but as the gyrations that have taken place between 1865 and the early twenty-first century in the way the American Civil War has been remembered painfully illustrate, it turns out that it is actually quite easy for nations or groups to "revise" and "rewrite" their collective memories. Since, as the great French historian Jacques Le Goff once remarked, "memory only seeks to rescue the past in order to serve the present and the future," it is hardly surprising that exercises in collective historical remembrance far more closely resemble myth on one side and political propaganda on the other than they do history, at least as that is understood as an academic discipline—the kind of history that when done properly is always critical and whose insights, though they may from time to time be deemed useful to society as a whole, were not set out to instruct. In contrast, historical remembrance is generally considered valuable insofar as it is of service to society.

Our understanding of memory as a social construct goes back to the 1920s and derives in large measure from the pioneering work of the French sociologist Maurice Halbwachs, the most gifted of Émile Durkheim's disciples.[1] Halbwachs would almost certainly have found the late-modern claim that everything, from human sexuality to our understanding of our historical traditions, is socially constructed both unoriginal and largely self-evident. What mainly interested him was the reconstruction rather than the deconstruction of how societies "remember." More specifically, in the words of the American sociologist Lewis Coser, Halbwachs understood collective memory as "a reconstruction of the past in the light of the present." Halbwachs derived much of his theory on group memory formation from the British neurologist Henry Head's studies of World War I veterans who had suffered head wounds. "What [someone with aphasia] lacks," Halbwachs wrote, "is less memories themselves than the framework in which to situate them." Obviously there is no such thing physiologically as collective memory, but what Halbwachs understood was that this does not make it any less of a sociological reality in which, to use the historian Horst Möller's gloss on Halbwachs's argument, "collective consciousness applied to memory results in *collective memory,*" memories that, in turn, "mold social groups, generations, and nations and constitute *identity.*"

Halbwachs was keenly aware of how costly the process could be. For while, as he put it, "The various groups that

1. Halbwachs had a long and distinguished academic career. In 1944, he was awarded the chair in social psychology at the Collège de France. A few months later, he was arrested by the Gestapo and died of hunger and dysentery in Buchenwald in 1945. Jorge Semprún, a fellow prisoner with him there, wrote an extraordinary account of Halbwachs's death in his memoir *Literature or Life.*

compose society are capable at every moment of reconstructing their past," at the same time that "they reconstruct it, they deform it." But for all its brilliance and originality, Halbwachs's work never sought to address why, both politically and morally, some of these "reconstructions" and "rewritings" have proven to be harmful or at least far riskier than others at given points in history but then later evolve or are transformed (the mechanisms that make this happen are rarely straightforward) into phenomena that pose little or no danger to the societies and polities to which they were once so toxic.

To say that collective memory is a social construct, however, tells us little or nothing about the moral character of such remembrance. The proof of this, as Le Goff has pointed out, is that even in the present golden age of collective memory, commemorations of the past were never more common than in Hitler's Germany and Mussolini's Italy (one might add Lenin and Stalin's Russia and Mao's China). And certainly if Coser's rendering of Halbwachs's thesis is right, and memory needs "continuous feeding from collective sources and is sustained by social and moral props," then if the morality of those sources is tainted, the memories being created or solidified will be poisonous as well.

These are extreme cases and as such are almost certainly less instructive than they may appear (though doubtless they perform a pedagogic service for those who continue to believe that remembrance is always positive). The more difficult cases are those in which a particular set of "constructed" collective memories serves to foment or exacerbate anger and conflict at one moment in time and then, a few generations later, is not only seen as harmless but is enlisted in the diametrically opposed mission of palliating the culture of grievance that appealing to such forms of remembrance once nurtured.

Irish history provides a particularly illuminating case study of the uses and misuses of the past in the construction, reconstruction, amendment, and transformation of the collective memory.

That the mythical Ireland still to be found in the frozen republicanism of a declining portion of the Irish diaspora and in the clichés of the Irish National Tourist Board never really existed—any more than the mythical France of baguettes and reason, the mythical United States as humankind's last best hope, or the mythical China as the only significant civilization in the world existed—should not need stating. But what to make of what the Irish historian John M. Regan has called the foundation-myth of the Irish state that venerated Irish history as "the immemorial struggle against English misrule, . . . eulogized physical-force and honored the pieties of separatist republican-nationalism . . . [and] was rooted in quasi-religious representations enveloping the republican rebellion or 'rising' of Easter 1916?" While obviously many Irish people never believed anything of the sort, and many so-called revisionist Irish historians tried to modulate and modify it, between Irish independence in 1921 and the so-called Celtic Tiger economic boom of the late 1990s and early 2000s followed by the crash of 2008,[2] the dominant strain of collective memory in Ireland (and even more strongly in the Irish diaspora) nonetheless remained anchored in what the Irish literary critic Declan Kilberd has called "the old morality-tale of Holy Ireland versus Perfidious Albion." This was confirmed institutionally by the political domination over Irish life for the first seventy-five years

2. As Fintan O'Toole, a fierce critic of the Ireland of the boom, has pointed out, it at least liberated the Irish from the crushing weight of historical memory.

of the state by one political party, Fianna Fáil, that saw itself as the inheritor of the "spirit" of Easter 1916.

It was this mix of Fenianism and Catholicism, along with a particular variant of Irish cultural nationalism with its emphasis on the Irish language incarnated by one of the leaders of the Easter Rising, Patrick Pearse, and the rejection of Irish political parties seeking Home Rule for Ireland by peaceful means, that would for most of the history of the Republic of Ireland become what the Irish historian R. F. Foster has called the country's "received wisdom" about its own history. In reality, though, what Foster once described as "Pearse's particular ideology of blood-sacrifice and mystical Catholicism" represented only one strain of nineteenth- and early-twentieth-century Irish nationalism, and a narrower strain of the Irish cultural revival between the late 1880s and the beginning of the First World War. As Foster has shown in his *Vivid Faces: The Revolutionary Generation in Ireland, 1890–1923,* many held views that could not have been farther from Pearse's, and were committed to what Foster has described elsewhere as "an opening out of attitudes, a modernization of nationalism, an exploration of cultural diversity, [and] a questioning of too-readily-received forms of authority in public and indeed private life." Foster even speculates at the end of *Vivid Faces* that for many members of the revolutionary generation, the revolution they made "may not have been the revolution they intended, or wanted"—a historical fate hardly unique to Irish revolutionaries.

Even leaving aside the ways that the central cultural and social questions such as religious faith and sexuality were framed at the time in Ireland and focusing solely on politics, the consensus among Irish historians today is that the shift of the center of gravity of Irish nationalism from parliamentary politics to the Romantic cultural nationalism of the Gaelic

Revival and the armed resistance of the Irish Volunteers, the military wing of the Irish Republican Brotherhood, occurred in large measure because of the political failure of Irish constitutional nationalism, in which the best option for Ireland was seen as Home Rule within the British state system. Pearse might still have denounced the Home Rulers' leader in 1916, John Redmond, for "untruth and blasphemy . . . the mumblings and gibberings of lost souls," but had not Redmond's predecessor as leader of the Irish Parliamentary Party, Charles Stewart Parnell, been brought down by sexual scandal in 1890, the collective memory in Ireland of what was at the heart of Irish nationalism might well have been different.

Instead, however, the idea that there had been a symbiotic relationship between the political and military goals of the Easter Rising and the cultural ambitions of the Gaelic Revival, and that taken together these represented the collective goal of the people of Ireland, came to be so central to the collective understanding of Irish nationalism that in *Ulysses* James Joyce could invent a nationalist conversation in Barney Kiernan's pub in which the politics are overwhelmingly cultural and revolve around "Irish sports and shoneen games the like of lawn tennis and about hurley and putting the stone and racy of the soil and building up a nation once again."

None of this is "historical." No one in the milieu Joyce drew on for nationalist characters in *Ulysses* imagined that it was possible to re-create the clan-based Irish nation that had existed before Cromwell's slaughter of the Irish or, going still farther back, Henry VIII's unseating of the Fitzgerald dynasty. Nor would Joyce's republicans have wanted to, for that matter. What was of concern to them, as has generally been the case for cultural nationalists whether in Ireland or elsewhere, was the trauma of the Irish nation's destruction and the heady prospect of being able to breathe life back into it. At first glance, the rhetoric accompanying this appears to be highly specific, as when, to return to Joyce's archetypal rendering, "Irish" sports such as hurley are described as the antitheses of shoneen ones (the word is a derogatory description of Irish people who prefer English attitudes and styles). But in historical terms, these memories of the past are as imprecise and, in some cases, as anachronistic as they are impassioned. Crucially, there is absolutely no room for ambiguity. And yet as Foster has said about Irish history (and as with "his" revolutionaries' disenchantment with their revolution, this is true of a number of other nations as well), its ambiguities "are, in many ways, the most distinctive thing about it."

But as Foster himself certainly knows, even if he is right, that is beside the point in the sense that the essence of historical remembrance consists of identification and psychological proximity rather than historical accuracy, let alone historical nuance and depth. Perhaps this is what led Foster in one of his best essays, "Theme-Parks and Histories," to declare that he had some sympathy for the Northern Irish critic Edna Longley's suggestion that the next commemoration of Irish history "might take the form of raising a monument to Amnesia, and forgetting where we put it." As a historian, Foster wrote, "I have to be rather shocked by the idea. But as an Irishman I am rather attracted to it."

Irony aside, the question of whether historical remembrance is constructed, imagined, manufactured out of whole cloth, or willed into being is of profound importance to professional historians—not least because, as Möller has observed, they "know that myths and legends can be as historically important and politically potent as reality, if they happen to match a society's expectations at a given point in time." But as the best historians realize, the more important collective memory is for a society, the less likely they themselves are to be heeded. And this is leaving aside the question Claude Lévi-Strauss was inviting the profession to consider when he asked whether "when we try to do scientific history, do we really do something scientific, or do we too remain astride our own mythology?"

What both professional historians and the general public agree on is that, as the nineteenth-century (nationalist) French historian Ernest Renan put it, nations are founded "on a rich legacy of memories." Or, in the sociologist Dominique Schnapper's more modern formulation, "For individuals and peoples alike, memory is the predicate of self." In Renan's case, although he was himself a superb archival researcher, a master of both written and material sources, he did not call for such memories to be based on the best available historical research. To the contrary, he was adamantly opposed to letting the historical chips fall where they may. "Forgetting," he wrote in *What Is a Nation?* (1882), "and I would even say historical error, is an essential factor in the creation of a nation."

And far from welcoming "the progress of historical studies," Renan insisted that it often posed "a danger to [the sense of] nationhood." Taken out of context, this may seem more romantic than it actually was. For Renan was under no illusions: "Nations," he wrote, "are not something eternal. They had their beginnings and they will end." (Presciently, he foresaw the eventual replacement of nation-states such as France and Germany by what he called a "European Confederation.") Given this eventual fate, and given that Renan understood the continued existence of a nation as being based on what he called a "daily plebiscite"—the risk of disintegration that it faces from its beginning to its end—Renan insisted that, if called upon to choose, a nation would be well advised to opt for myth, codified in collective remembrance, over history.

It is a tribute to Renan's influence that his contention that a nation is "a large-scale solidarity" remains, whether implicitly or explicitly, the dominant view not only of most countries' elites but of ordinary citizens as well. Were this not the case, other than invoking the old Marxist dogma of "false consciousness," it would make no sense that the increasingly common attempts to debunk or even modify collective national myths have so often provoked such alarm. An extreme example of this, in the instance that shared myths guaranteed democracy and shattering them represented an existential danger to it, was the suggestion in 1971 by the Irish political scientist Brian Farrell that "once the myth of the state is questioned extra-constitutional methods become valid." A less apocalyptic iteration of this view is that while coherent and persuasive collective memory may be able to be formed with little regard for historical accuracy (a case can be made that, indeed, such indifference is a sine qua non of such projects), too much critical history can undermine the consensus over what societies need to recall and what they need to forget if their cohesion and their citizens' sense of mutual solidarity and, probably more important, allegiance to the state is to be maintained. Or, to put it another way, can a sense of national belonging endure if pride in a nation's history is undermined by the wide dissemination of those elements of the historical record Renan was convinced needed to be ignored or forgotten?

We are far removed from scholarly debate here. For not only are we not talking about history, we are not even talking about memory in any proper sense, but rather about morality, ideology, and, often, the intellectual raw materials for cultural and political mobilizations. To insist on the point is not to assert that the claims of collective memory are equally powerful at all times in all places, or are necessarily always compelling even in countries such as Ireland where the authority of nationalism has run so deep for so long. Writing of his own childhood in the 1930s and the early to mid-1940s, for example, the Irish writer John McGahern could affirm that "the 1916 Rising was not considered to be of any great importance in the country I grew up in." Because Easter 1916 had occurred comparatively recently, he explained, "it probably was too close in time for the comfort of mythmaking."

But at other times, the need for the security that such mythmaking affords can seem desperately important. For example, large numbers of people in the United States today care passionately about whether American schoolchildren should continue to be taught, as they have been since the founding of the republic, that Columbus was the heroic discoverer of America or whether instead, as at least some U.S. schoolchildren are now being taught, he should be portrayed as a brutal and amoral servant of the Spanish Empire intent on despoiling a continent whose location he could not even correctly identify.

It might be more convenient for those who favor the revisionist version if those who insist that the traditional view of Columbus must continue to prevail were know-nothings who were either unable or unwilling to face historical reality. But the matter is hardly so simple, and there is plenty of anecdotal evidence that suggests that what most worries those who favor the retention of the traditional curriculum is the possibility (some would say the inevitability) that if the old consensus is repudiated, not only will Americans no longer understand how to take pride in their nation's origins, many will be tempted to repudiate its present as well. In a country of immigrants, an increasing proportion of whom have arrived within the past decade and still maintain ties with their nations of origin via the Internet that would have been impossible even half a century earlier, such concerns are defensible. Nor are they restricted to the United States. The early twenty-first century has turned out to be one of the great periods of global mass migration in modern history. Given this unanticipated version of the Americanization of at least the rich world, it should come as no surprise that similar "education wars" are raging all over the Global North.

The case of Australia is especially illuminating. During the late 1990s and early 2000s, John Howard's conservative government made a concerted effort to blunt what it viewed as the inroads of a leftist "multicultural" view of the country's history, one that the Australian center right and right believed wildly overemphasized Australia's mistreatment of its indigenous peoples. By accentuating the crimes and failures of the Australian state and Australian society over its positive accomplishments, conservatives believed that the multiculturalists were depriving new immigrants, the majority of whom now came from Asia and the Middle East rather than, as in the past, Europe, of the chance to be integrated into the Australian national "family." The multiculturalists, Howard claimed, had espoused a "black armband" view of history, and even their putative accomplishments—above all in recognizing the sufferings and celebrating the accomplishments of marginalized populations, especially the country's Aboriginal peoples—sooner or later would be dwarfed by the social discord they would engender and the national disunity they would sow.

We do not have to accept Howard's prescriptions to recognize that some prominent Australian multiculturalists have left themselves open to the charges he leveled at them; political positions aside, their indifference to, not to say disdain for, the historical record can be breathtaking. An emblematic figure in this is the University of Melbourne academic Chris Healy. He has called for new histories to be written of the story of Eliza

Fraser—a European woman who, after having been shipwrecked along the Queensland coast in 1836, lived with the Ngulung-bara people for some years before being found by a settler search party. Healy's proposal might seem reasonable were it not for the fact that he went on to insist that these new works would need to "eschew a desire to rescue an authentic Eliza Fraser." And Healy was anything but the only prominent Australian multiculturalist to treat history with such disdain.

However, it is important not to exaggerate, as so many conservatives, and by no means only in Australia, often do, the existential dangers to our societies that this crass form of multiculturalism poses. Bitter as these history wars often are, the experience of the past century in the United States, Canada, Australia, and western Europe shows that not only do all such cultural conflicts end at some point but that, whether explicitly or implicitly, they invariably end in some form of compromise in which elements of the older and newer conceptions of the national past are joined. In any case, even were such "historic compromises" to prove impossible to arrive at, it is an illusion to imagine that collective historical myths remain fixed for more than a few generations; viewed from a longer perspective, they eventually mutate, often out of all recognition from where they started. As Frances FitzGerald put it in *America Revised,* her history of American history textbooks from the nineteenth century to the late 1970s (when her book was published), "These works are consensus documents . . . themselves a part of history in that they reflect the concerns, the conventional wisdom, and even the fads of the age that produced them."

And at some point, the reigning pieties, whatever they are, begin to ring hollow. In 1918, when Lytton Strachey published *Eminent Victorians,* his series of debunking portraits of four of the great iconic figures of Victorian England—General Charles

"Chinese" Gordon, Florence Nightingale, Henry Cardinal Manning, and Thomas Arnold—the historical facts he uncovered were scarcely new, nor were his arguments particularly convincing from a scholarly perspective. To the contrary, in the words of the old Oxbridge joke, "what was true wasn't new, and what was new wasn't true." If the book found a receptive audience, it was largely because, in the last days of the First World War, the myths and memorial pieties of the prewar era had been completely undermined and discredited by the slaughter on the Western Front and in the Middle East, at Gallipoli and Kut, and the British public was ready for a radical revision of what, with apologies to those involved in the education wars, might be called the established canon of collective memory.

In his introduction to *The Invention of Tradition,* the pathbreaking book he edited with Terrence Ranger in 1983, Eric Hobsbawm wrote of what he called "new traditions" being established "when a rapid transformation of society weakens or destroys the social pattern for which 'old' traditions had been designed." One of the most startling cases described in the book is that of the Highland tradition in Scotland, particularly in its sartorial expressions such as the kilt and "clan tartans." The former appears to have been invented in the 1720s by an English Quaker from Lancashire, Thomas Rawlinson, while the latter did not exist in their modern form until the 1750s. *The Invention of Tradition* focuses on Britain and the British Empire, but as Hobsbawm pointed out in his introduction, similar phenomena are to be found in many if not most countries. The white southern women who began forming Ladies' Memorial Associations soon after the end of the Civil War are one example of this. As Caroline Janney has put it, these associations "succeeded in creating memorial tributes and traditions that intensified existing emotional attachment to the Confederate cause."

There can be little doubt that the efforts of the southern women's organizations were crucial to creating collective memories among white southerners that were extremely damaging to the nation both morally and politically. Yet when Horst Möller, writing of Europe at the end of the Second World War, insists that both "the individual memories of individual Europeans and the collective memory of nations could not remain as they had been," we sympathize with his view. Whether we can call the collective memory of the white American South an instance of the abuse of memory and the transformation of post-1945 European remembrance an example of memory's appropriate use (as the French philosopher Tzvetan Todorov, who used *The Abuses of Memory* as the title for a fascinating small book on the subject, presumably would) is a key question, and its answer is far less morally self-evident than is commonly supposed.

How does collective memory function? To understand this, the political scientist Benedict Anderson's template of the "imagined community" is invaluable. The distinctions that need to be drawn between how history and memory operate and the different ends they serve are by themselves insufficient. What the study of the engineering of traditions and the model of the national as an imagined community help clarify is the extent to which collective historical remembrance falls between history and memory, in a sense using both instrumentally without being a great respecter of either.

Whatever its purposes, the authority of collective memory depends, as Renan understood, on our not inquiring too insistently about its factuality and not worrying overmuch about its contingency, but instead allowing ourselves to be swept away by a strong emotion dressed up in the motley of historical fact. Typologically, it matters little whether the feeling in question is one of solidarity, of mourning, of love of one's own nation or disenchantment with it, or of hatred for another's nation or envy of it. Where remembrance is concerned, it would seem that it is Nietzsche who has the last word: "There are no facts, only interpretations."

What are the dangers here? The most obvious is that, too often, the suspension of disbelief required to keep faith with such collective self-conceptions has proved to be far more costly humanly and politically than is commonly assumed. The Oxford historian Timothy Garton Ash once asserted confidently in an interview that just as "a person without a memory is a child," so "a national or any political community without memory is likely to be childish." But it is anything but self-evident that this is true. Empirically there is much to support the contrary argument: in many parts of the world it is not the relinquishing but the holding on to memories that seems to make societies childish. And in societies in which there is a real risk of fragmentation or worse, invoking certain memories can sometimes resemble nothing so much as the proverbial yelling of "Fire!" in a crowded theater.

The crucial point is this: we do not have to deny the value of memory to insist that the historical record (the verifiable one, not the mythopoeic one) does not justify the moral free pass that remembrance is usually accorded today. Collective historical memory, and the forms of remembrance that are its most common expression, are neither factual, nor proportional, nor stable. To be sure, were the political implications of this largely positive or, failing that, at least largely neutral, then arguing for a more skeptical view of remembrance would be both disrespectful to all those people to whom it provides strength and solace, and unnecessary. But is this the case?

Presumably, Timothy Garton Ash would insist that it is. "Memory," he has said, "is a vital part of building a European identity," and he has been critical of the inroads that what he has described as the American understanding of history as something relatively unimportant have made into the central and eastern European view of its significance. But the strength of the U.S. model, and the problematic character of the one Garton Ash has championed, have been brutally exposed by the hostility with which the Central and Eastern European countries to which he refers have reacted to the arrival of more than one million refugees and economic migrants from Syria, Iraq, Afghanistan, sub-Saharan Africa, and Bangladesh and Pakistan in 2015, and to the very real prospect that they are the "advance guard" of migrant flows that will soon increase to many millions. And however politically incorrect it may be to point this out, if memory is an essential element to building a European identity, then the arrival of masses of people who share none of these memories, and, more to the point, bring with them extra-European memories of their own, will unquestionably make the project Garton Ash espouses at the very least a great deal more difficult in the near and medium term, and may perhaps force a radical rethinking by Europeans of the role of memory in the definition of what it means to be European in the twenty-first century.

In contrast, an Australian or a New Zealander, each coming from a society that, on balance, has made a successful transition from monocultural to multicultural societies, might understandably react to my notes of caution by demanding to know what could be wrong with wearing a poppy in one's lapel on Anzac Day or Remembrance Day. Part of the reply to this is that nothing is wrong with it: it is an entirely appropriate and decent thing to do precisely because people in Australia and New Zealand do not wear poppies in their lapels on all the other days of the year, and that the significance of the gesture would be very different if they did. Such blanket displays are scarcely unknown. Think for example of the significance in the United States of wearing an American flag lapel pin. Whatever the original intention behind wearing it was, such pins rapidly became emblems of the American right, ubiquitous on Fox News though rarely seen on the other major networks. But the gesture so resonated with the U.S. public that only a few years later not wearing the pins left a politician open to the charge of being unpatriotic, and as a result many liberal American senators and representatives started wearing them as well to rebuff such charges. This group included Barack Obama, who only began to do so when in 2007, while still a U.S. senator, he launched his campaign for the presidency.

Memory can be used as a political litmus test, for good causes and bad ones alike, in much the same way as a lapel pin bearing the image of the national flag (the practice is now no longer exclusively American) is used. If we assume that this is the case, then the question for those who insist, as Garton Ash does, on the link between weak collective memories and weak collective identities, is whether this is always a bad thing and if so, why? It should go without saying that there are no easy or definitive answers to this. Nietzsche wrote, "The question of the degree to which life requires the service of history at all is one of the supreme questions and concerns in regard to the health of a man, a people, or a culture." To offer two extreme examples, one can agree with Möller that "the culture of memory [in Germany after 1945] is one of the great moral, political and societal achievements of the Federal Republic of Germany," as has been demonstrated most recently by the humane welcome Angela Merkel's conservative government in Berlin has afforded to the masses of refugees and migrants for whom Germany stands as a modern-day promised land. But would one not say, and not just in light of the slaughter at the Emanuel African Methodist Episcopal Church in Charleston, that the culture of memory of many white southerners from the Confederates' surrender at Appomattox in 1865 to the present day is one of the great moral, political, and societal failures of the United States?

The example of the American South is anything but unique. I remember going to Belgrade in 1993 to visit Vuk Drašković, the Serb nationalist politician and writer who was then leading the mass opposition against the Slobodan Milošević regime, and had drawn liberal as well as ultra-nationalist support in Serbia for his cause. As I was leaving his office, my head still ringing with Drašković's romantic paeans of praise for the Chetnik leader Draža Mihailović, one of his young aides pressed a folded bit of paper into my hand. It turned out to be blank except for a date: 1453—the year Orthodox Constantinople fell to the Muslim Ottomans. Friends of mine who had worked in the former Yugoslavia during the Croatian and Bosnian wars had similar experiences in Zagreb and Sarajevo, though the dates in question were different. It certainly seemed as if the "sores of history," as the Irish writer Hubert Butler once called them, remained unhealed more than half a millennium later— at least in the desperate, degraded atmosphere of that time and place.

There is a broader and more consequential lesson to be learned from this. It is that far too often collective historical memory as understood and deployed by communities, peoples, and nations—which, again, is always selective, more often than not self-serving, and historically anything but unimpeachable— has led to war rather than peace, to rancor and ressentiment (which increasingly appears to be the defining emotion of our age) rather than reconciliation, and to the determination to exact revenge rather than commit to the hard work of forgiveness.

This is what happened in the American South after 1865 and, while diminished, is still happening today; it blighted the former Yugoslavia in the 1990s. Today, it is endemic in Israel-Palestine, in Iraq and Syria, in the Hindu nationalist populism of India's Bharatiya Janata Party, which the government of Narendra Modi is systematically institutionalizing, and among jihadis and Islamists both in the Muslim world and in the Muslim diaspora in western Europe, North America, and Australia. To insist on this is emphatically not to suggest that there is an easy solution. On the contrary, it is probable that human beings' need for community, already compelling in times of peace and plenty, comes to feel like a psychic and moral necessity in troubled times. But at least let there be no turning a blind eye to the high price societies have paid and are continuing to pay for the solace of remembrance.

History is not a menu. You can't have the solidarity that a national myth helps form and sustain without the self-absorption, nor can you have the pride without the fear. Nor, despite all the loose talk about globalization, is the universal ethical community that in his fine study *The Ethics of Memory* the Israeli philosopher Avishai Margalit has called for—here echoing Kant's vision of a worldwide civil society administering universal rights—anything other than a pipe dream, at least for now.

Margalit is certainly correct in concluding that if we could create what he calls a shared moral memory based on some generally accepted moral minima, there could be a globalization of conscience on a par in the ethical sphere with the globalization of capitalism and of migration. Yet he does not satisfactorily address the problem raised by the scholar of cultural reporting Susie Linfield of what such collective remembering by "humanity as a whole" would mean. "Why, and how," she asks, should "[a victim] of the Rwandan genocide remember those of the

Gulag? And why should a comfortable 25-year-old citizen of, say, Amsterdam—or Cairo or Beijing—remember either?" Margalit himself concedes that creating and legitimating the shared moral memory he is calling for will be extraordinarily difficult. But having set out the daunting character of the task, he then in effect falls back on the old German idealist view that holds that if something should be done, if it is truly a moral imperative, then it must be done—the world as "cosmological idea," to deploy another Kantian formulation. This injunction can be summarized in the formula "ought implies can."

In a time in which universal values seem to be under assault everywhere, even as, paradoxically, our era is increasingly defined by mass migrations on a scale not seen in generations and from much wider geographical sources than seen in centuries, this scarcely seems likely. There is even a whiff of eschatology about it: "Alle Menschen werden Brüder" (all men become brothers), The End. Even more problematically, Margalit's vision of the future is too close to the old fantasy of world government—a moral analogue to Esperanto that is admirable, but when all is said and done is a waste of hope. As the philosopher and historian Leszek Kolakowski once remarked, "We can imagine a universal brotherhood of wolves but not of humans, since the needs of wolves are limited and definable and therefore conceivably satisfied, whereas human needs have no boundaries we could delineate."

For better or worse, how we weigh the human need for remembrance against remembrance's dangers must take place in the context of how we live now and who we are as human beings. "In the terrifying time in which we live and create," wrote the exemplary historian of Judaism Yosef Yerushalmi, "eternity is not our immediate concern." Nor do we live in a world that, even were it to be transformed into a less terrifying place (which in the age of global warming and Daesh [also known as ISIS] hardly seems likely), ever will be converted to idealistic Kantian absolutism. Our challenge is different: to keep our bearings in a world in which, too often for it to be dismissed as a limiting case, values have proven to be incommensurable.

An obvious example of this is the often though by no means always inimical relationship in the aftermath of savage wars among three virtuous goals—truth, justice, and peace. This is especially relevant to the increasing number of conflicts in which there is no clear victor. In such circumstances, often what is needed is appeasement in its denotative sense of "soothing" or "bringing peace," though since the word has become so identified with Neville Chamberlain and Édouard Daladier in Munich in 1938 caving in to Hitler over Czechoslovakia, another term would have to be found. To achieve such appeasement will require some version of what the British philosopher John Gray has described as a modus vivendi among civilizations, cultures, religions, and nations. Far from political remembrance being always a moral imperative, then, there will be times when such remembrance is what stands in the way.

THREE

What Is Collective Memory Actually Good For?

O ld men forget, as Shakespeare has the king say in *Henry V.* But left to their own devices, societies forget too, and far more quickly than they used to. This "acceleration of history," as the French historian Daniel Halévy dubbed it, has been recognized since at least the latter part of the eighteenth century, and is the product both of the scientific revolutions of the previous century and of the intellectual and philosophical revolution that was the Enlightenment that culminated in the American and French Revolutions. In both its original and its subsequent forms, conceiving of history as something that accelerates, or even—as two of the central figures of the French Revolution, Condorcet and Robespierre, believed, for all that divided them—that can be *made* to accelerate, is inseparable from the idea of progress, which itself is a concept that historically only slightly predates the Enlightenment. Indeed, the historian Hugh Trevor-Roper once described the idea of progress as a seventeenth-century heresy.

In the orthodox Christian view, as Trevor-Roper noted, progress is simply not possible. History has a trajectory all right, running from the Creation to the Last Judgment, but as the French historian Frédéric Rouvillois put it in his pathbreaking *Invention of Progress, 1680 to 1730,* any history of human progress, particularly if one agrees with Halévy that such progress is constantly accelerating, is antithetical to the "linearity of the history of Salvation." That, after all, is the point the preacher in Ecclesiastes 1:2 is making when he declares, "Vanity of vanities, all is vanity." In Rouvillois's words, for the believer waiting for the end of days when God will judge if he or she is to be damned or saved, "progress is *impossible,* most importantly because it is *useless.*" As it says in John 12:31: "Now is the judgment of this world, now shall the prince of this world be cast out."

But one does not have to be a believer to find the idea of progress far-fetched. What for lack of better terms, and for all their imprecision and oversimplification, we call premodern or traditional societies may be better off during a given historical period than they were in a previous one—for example, because of good weather that leads to fuller harvests, or following success in war. But they may also find themselves worse off, should, say, they suffer famine (which they would have been likely to do given that it is a catastrophe that had afflicted all societies for all of recorded time until the second half of the twentieth century, when for the first time in human history they began to wane) or military defeat. Since the Enlightenment, the essence of the idea of progress has been that however difficult it may be to achieve in any given realm of human activity or of the human condition, it is at once inevitable and inexorable, rather than contingent and reversible, as it is in traditional societies. This is because, as Rouvillois writes at the end of his study, "Once one has adopted an optimistic conception of human history and one has affirmed the *reality* of progress, then one draws from one's sense that it is *necessary* the confidence that it will thus be *perpetual.*"

To insist on this point is not to claim that things never change in traditional cultures, the majority of which have been peasant cultures. Obviously they do, but usually so slowly that these changes are imperceptible to each generation. But the slowness of the change is not so much because such societies are governed by custom and precedent since, after all, this is also the purpose that, once successfully established, invented traditions are meant to serve. Rather, it is because, as Hobsbawm emphasized in his essay on the invention of tradition, there is so little demand in traditional societies for rapid change—again, except in extremis, as in cases where famine drives people from the countryside to the city, where they find that the older traditions are no longer fit for the purpose, and thus have to be either radically modified or jettisoned entirely.

The link between Halévy's "acceleration" and Hobsbawm's "invention of tradition" is that, as Hobsbawm put it in 1983, "[Large and rapid] changes have been particularly significant in the past 200 years, and it is therefore reasonable to expect these instant formalizations of new traditions to cluster during this period." Once the stable arrangements that began to come apart at the time of the Industrial Revolution had eroded past a certain point, they could never again be reconstituted. But few human beings can live without any traditions to which to adhere. As a result, when any real continuity with the past became impossible, that past had to be reimagined and reconstructed both for the present's and for the future's sake.

In the past fifty years, the acceleration has been particularly extreme in the hard sciences and technology, certainly, but also in the arts. The philosopher Karl Popper's dictum that the essential difference between the sciences and the humanities is that in the former propositions are empirically falsifiable whereas in the latter they are not is over-broad. It is true that historically innovation has played a more important role in Western art than it did in African, Indian, Southeast Asian, or Chinese art. Nonetheless, the divorce of the art of the present from the art of the past is all but absolute, and in this sense seems more radical than previous moments of rupture. The mental stance of the contemporary artist strikingly parallels that of the scientist in that the art of the past is deemed to be as irrelevant to the art of the present as pre-Copernican physics is deemed to be to string theory or trepanning to brain surgery.

The scientists and technologists are on firmer ground. One does not have to endorse the techno-utopianism of a Ray Kurzweil, or share Bill and Melinda Gates's conviction, which has informed all the work of their foundation—by far the richest in the history of philanthropy—that disease, hunger, and poverty will be all but ended or at least radically reduced thanks to technological innovation, to appreciate how much the world has changed, and how much that change continues to accelerate.[1] In the early twenty-first century, and in every domain except our identities as mortal, biological beings (though Ray Kurzweil and other like-minded cyber-utopians in Silicon Valley would reject even that caveat), the transformation continues. For the first time in human history, a majority of the world's population lives in cities instead of in the countryside. The free movement of capital is taken for granted, as is the alternative, borderless geography of cyberspace. And all the while, the

---

1. Scientific progress is no myth. But as John Gray has written, "The myth is that the progress achieved in science and technology can occur in ethics, politics, or, more simply, civilization."

unprecedented movement of poor people from the Global South toward the Global North, which is an accelerator of history if ever there was one, and which may be able to be managed but certainly cannot be stopped, is hollowing out national identities even as it makes a mockery of national borders.

And if what in Spanish is called *mestizaje* (the term has cultural and historical connotations that makes it far more resonant than its English translation "the mixing of the races") is proceeding apace, so is global cultural and linguistic homogenization. Not a year goes by without at least ten small languages dying out, while small cultures are being steadily subsumed into a few dominant ones, largely articulated in Chinese, Spanish, English, Arabic, Hindi, Bengali, and to some extent French and Portuguese. Climate change, even if the rise in global temperatures is held to a (comparatively) manageable range of between 2 and 2.5 degrees Celsius rather than a catastrophic 3.5- to 5-degree range, will transform cultures as surely as it will transform the environment. And scientists are now convinced that the earth has entered the sixth wave of mass extinctions of plants and animals in the past half-billion years and predict that a quarter or more of all land species will no longer exist by the year 2050. In short, the historical stresses that led to the accelerated manufacture of traditions that Hobsbawm and Ranger identified are only a foretaste of those the world is subject to now, let alone what we are likely to confront in the future.

Narrowing the frame to politics, the acceleration of history template is particularly useful when applied to those periods when empires fall and new polities rise or are revived, or when the demography of a given society is altered so dramatically that emphasizing a historical consensus that is no longer shared by a preponderance of the state's citizens no longer makes sense. Historically, this question has been especially bedeviling to settler societies such as the United States, Canada, and Australia, though the recent huge immigration to western European countries has blurred the differences between settler and nonsettler, virtually guaranteeing that most of the nations of the European Union will soon be confronting similar challenges. In the United States, for example, when the overwhelming majority of Americans were of European origin, what even in the age of the European colonial empires at their zenith in global terms was certainly a disproportionate emphasis on the history of Europe was defensible. But in the increasingly de-Europeanized United States of today it is not. The problem, of course, is what to replace it with.

Timothy Garton Ash has suggested that a possible approach to the challenges facing a European Union now expanded to twenty-seven countries is not to try to forge a common collective memory, for, as he rightly observed, one would "have to do extreme violence to the historical truth" in order to do so. Instead, Garton Ash proposed defining European identity as "nations that are coming from very different histories but aspiring toward shared goals." Yet as Garton Ash undoubtedly understands as well as anyone, "shared goals" are hard enough to define in good times, and these are anything but good times in Europe. The Greek crisis alone, but also the rise of populist parties on both the left (Syriza in Greece, Podemos in Spain, and others) and on the right (the Front National in France and the Danish People's Party, for example), the inability of European governments to agree on how to craft a common policy on the resettlement of the latest waves of migrants, and the cultural, political, and economic panic, whether justified or not (probably both, in my view), that the refugee exodus has caused offer ample evidence that the era in which serious thinkers such as Garton Ash and Jürgen Habermas could continue to believe that the humane vision of statesmen such as Jean Monnet, Robert Schuman,

Paul-Henri Spaak, and Emile Noël for Europe and its vocation in the world still enjoyed a preponderance of support from the European public may well be ending, if it has not ended already.

But let us assume that Habermas's anxieties that the European project is in the process of being transformed into the opposite of what its founders had intended, and that the world's "first transnational democracy [risks becoming] an especially effective, because disguised, arrangement for exercising a kind of post-democratic rule," are misplaced. And let us hope that enough hearts and heads are swayed by Garton Ash's fierce and eloquent response to the reaction of the vice president of the European Commission to Syriza's election victory in January 2015 ("We don't change policies depending on elections") when he wrote, "Given the choice between democracy and a paternalistic, top-down, Euro-Leninist version of European integration, I will choose democracy every time." Even assuming such a positive outcome, the success of the European project will remain in doubt.

The reasons for this have been brilliantly analyzed by the French political scientist Zaki Laïdi in his *A World Without Meaning: The Crisis of Meaning in International Politics.* "If in Western societies," he writes, "the social and political forces which claim to be the paradigm of the transformation are in crisis, it is precisely because identity transmission and social transformation seem disconnected. Transmission is thought old-fashioned (nationalism) and transformation destructive (globalization), whereas transmission ought to be made positive and transformation protective."

If anything, Laïdi understates the problem, especially that of transmission, since today even to speak of a common European, or, for that matter, American or Australian, identity is problematic. This is at least in part because, as the Dutch

academic Joep Leerssen has pointed out, "Historical investigation has turned from victors and triumphant elites to the
downtrodden, the persecuted, the victimized." Instead of commemorations of shared trauma in what Leerssen calls "the
Binyon/Tennyson mode of transmuting loss and grief into
edification and catharsis," remembrance largely inhabits a
"'never again' mode." Garton Ash's prescription for Europeans
to explore "the diversity of our memories" in order to arrive at
shared goals simply takes insufficient account of the degree to
which the new politics of commemoration is grounded in what
Leerssen calls the "experience of oppression, of defeat, of injustice and grievance" and informed by the idea that "the lesson to
be drawn from past injustice is one of vigilance and assertive-
ness." Meanwhile, those who continue to want the previous
consensus to prevail are furious at what they see as disloyalty
and ingratitude, particularly on the part of immigrant populations and sexual minorities. In our new era of ressentiment, the
idea of a shared anything seems increasingly out of reach.

But even if the divide were narrower between collective
memory in the service of national unity and collective memory
in the service of those victimized by the nation in question who
await at least an acknowledgment and often an apology for what
they or their ancestors have suffered, the new synthesis of the
two, no matter how satisfactory or unsatisfactory to both sides,
will be as mortal as any other set of political arrangements and
cultural compromises. If there is a puzzle in all this, it is that
anyone could believe that political arrangements could be
other than transitory, no matter how potent they might seem
at a particular moment in history. In a fascinating short memoir
called "Where Statues Go to Die," the historian of the British
Empire David Cannadine illustrated the fragility and contingency of even the most grandiose emblems of bygone empires

by describing how during a visit to India in 2003 he had come face to face with the inglorious fate of colonial monuments. He was taken to a large open space on the edge of New Delhi, where in colonial times British viceroys had held their great ceremonial gatherings known as "durbars." What Cannadine found was a "neglected, overgrown, obscure piece of ground" that conveyed the message that "earthly power is transient, and that imperial dominion is ephemeral."

In the remotest corner of the site, he describes being led to "a most astonishing scene: a dozen immense statues, rising up from the bushes and the brambles, like the chessmen arrayed for that terrifying contest towards the end of the first Harry Potter film." They were statues of George V, emperor of India, and a number of British viceroys, "placed by the British in New Delhi to be permanent monuments to men whose lives and deeds they deemed worthy of everlasting commemoration." But India had moved on—just as virtually every other former European colony, French, Dutch, Portuguese, or Spanish, where such statues once occupied pride of place has moved on. A brilliant Cartier-Bresson photograph taken in 1949 shows the official portraits of colonial officials being removed like so much rubbish from the governor's mansion in Jakarta shortly after Indonesia gained its independence from Holland. The journalist and writer Ryszard Kapuściński witnessed something similar in Angola in 1975. As he recounts it, the Portuguese colonists all but stripped their houses, crating up the contents to be loaded onto freighters that would take them from Luanda back to Portugal. But the colonists paid no heed to the colonial statuary, and soldiers of the victorious MPLA (Popular Movement for the Liberation of Angola) removed them from their plinths and carted them unceremoniously to a field much like the one David Cannadine had seen on the outskirts of New Delhi.

Such high, iconoclastic moments, when all the grand symbols of colonial rule reverted to what they had been when they were still being cast at the foundry—bits of hewn and polished stone now representing something barely intelligible—are hardly restricted to the public monuments and official portraits of European colonial officials. After 1989, many of the same sorts of scenes were played out throughout the Soviet Union, and again, a few years later, in the Balkans.[2] Somehow I doubt that Lenin or Stalin ever imagined, any more than Lord Curzon did, that his images would be transformed from symbols of domination to kitsch in a matter of decades.[3] And yet that is precisely what happened in Russia, to the point that the English-language *Moscow Times* could run a story in 1996 that set out the going prices in the "antique" shops along the Old Arbat for such objects as busts of Lenin and "a large plate in good condition of Stalin and Voroshilov at work."

Despite the comic turns these episodes can take, the underlying reality is deadly serious. For we are back with Kipling once more. He would certainly not have been surprised by what Cannadine saw in that field on the outskirts of New Delhi.

2. These could sometimes be comic. In Tirana, shortly after the fall of the Albanian regime, I visited a foundry most of whose work during the entire Communist period had been casting statues of party leaders, above all of Enver Hoxha, the country's dictator. When I met the works manager, though, he seemed remarkably cheerful. It turned out that the foundry was as busy as ever . . . making statues of Mother Teresa.

3. A strong case can be made that when such iconoclastic moments do *not* occur, a successful transition from one kind of society to another is less likely to be achieved. Had the federal authorities in Washington, D.C., been willing after Reconstruction to stop the widespread reemergence and official display throughout the South of Confederate flags and other symbols, the ideology of the Lost Cause might not have become dominant in the way that it did.

After all, for Kipling the mortality of every empire was as certain as our own individual mortality (and possibly even more so since, at the end of his life the poet had the uneasy consolation in believing in spirits as well as in Jesus Christ). Where empire was concerned, though, there could be no appeal. As it says in Psalms 146:3–4: "Put not your trust in princes, nor in the son of man, in whom there is no help. His breath goeth forth, he returneth to his earth; in that very day his thoughts perish."

That through all of this—"action and suffering, power and pride, sin and death," as Karl Löwith put it—God endured could offer no consolation to Kipling. He well understood that God is mainly outside history, intervening only at its beginning with the act of love that is the Creation, and at its end, the Apocalypse, which Leszek Kolakowski once described as the "never-ending framework of Jesus' preaching." Eschatology, not the future in this world, was what concerned many of the best known of the early Christian martyrs, such as Thecla, who vowed to remain a virgin and finally fled into the mountains, where she preached the Gospel until her death at ninety. Or Maximilla, whose love of God impelled her to pray for Him to intercede so that she would no longer have to have sex with her husband, Aegeates. How could these women have committed themselves to relinquishing all their property and have been so ambivalent even about having children had they not seen themselves as being betrothed to the world to come?

For the rest, game, set, and match to Shelley:

"My name is Ozymandias, King of Kings:
Look on my works, ye Mighty, and despair!"
Nothing beside remains. Round the decay
Of that colossal wreck, boundless and bare
The lone and level sands stretch far away.

Although he, too, despaired, Kipling still chose to write about forgetting in the conditional: "Lest we forget!" He was right to do so, for had he done anything else, his appeal for remembrance would have been rendered all but meaningless (imagine what Shelley would have done with the theme of "Recessional"). And remembrance is emphatically not meaningless except in the cognitively and probably ethically useless framework of eternity. Human beings are drawn to ceremony and, whether they are believers in a religion or not, to piety as well.[4] This is why, without falling into a subspecies of ancestor worship, surely there is something impious, or at the least ethically impoverished, about forgetting the sacrifices and the sufferings of those who came before. If those who died in battle or gave their lives for their beliefs are not remembered, how can their acts have any meaning? And for their sacrifices, read all sacrifice. In Dryden's great phrase, such a forgetting truly would be "the untuning of the sky."

"Imagine . . . a world without memories," runs the tagline on the website of the government-backed "Australian Memory of the World Register," part of a global project on memory organized by UNESCO. The effort is less doom-laden than these words might lead us to believe, and largely involves the preservation of historical documents and the recording of oral histories. But that does not make the admonition on the home page any less emblematic of the nonsense that so much of the discussion about memory seems to produce. Quite simply, the world does not have memories; nor do nations; nor do groups of people. Individuals remember, full stop. Yet in the early twenty-first century, collective memory is often spoken of as if

4. As John Gray has pointed out, the resurgence of religion in the twenty-first century is a global phenomenon. If anything, it may be atheism that proves to be the historical parenthesis.

it were indeed on a par with individual, which is to say genuine, memory, and not infrequently, though almost never explicitly, as if it morally outranked it.

To paraphrase the progressive leftist intellectual Randolph Bourne's sardonic remark about war, is collective memory now the health of state? Reading the literature on remembrance, one might very well think so. The fact that individuals forget, whether through the sad cognitive deficits that come with age or, conversely, some happy remission in their private life (such as fading of the memory of the lover who broke one's heart), is not thought to pose a threat to society as a whole. In contrast, a collective failure of remembrance is often presented as if it were an invitation to moral or political disaster. The paradigmatic contemporary expression of this is the commonly voiced assertion that shirking our moral obligation to remember the Shoah is for all intents and purposes to strike a blow against what Thomas Jefferson called "the decent opinions of mankind." A person who did so might not be an "assassin of memory," the term that the historian Pierre Vidal-Naquet rightly affixed to Holocaust deniers such as Robert Faurisson. But he or she has committed a grave ethical solecism just the same.

This sense underpins the views of Avishai Margalit. For him, the issue is not a matter of Jewish particularism, though because the Jews are a religion that became a people rather than a people who became a religion (the formulation is Harold Bloom's), the question of that particularism, and, more broadly, of a Jewish approach to history that is in many ways unique, must be addressed if one hopes to get to the heart of the matter. Karl Löwith thought that because Christians were not a historical people—"their solidarity [was] merely one of faith"—it was impossible to apply a purely Christian interpretation to the historical destiny of Christian peoples. But he argued that the

destiny of the Jewish people *was* a subject for Jewish interpretation, presumably up to and including the Shoah. Margalit,
though, is interested in global ethical minima: that is, in arriving
at a standard that should command not just one people's or even
one civilization's allegiance but humanity's as a whole. For he
believes—and to be clear, not as a matter of Jewish particularism—that there are certain "moral nightmares," as he calls them,
the Shoah first and foremost, that must remain in our collective
memories because they are "striking examples of radical evil
and crimes against humanity, such as enslavement, deportations
of civilian populations, and mass exterminations."

In effect, what Margalit is saying is that the need to be alert
to radical evil (he borrows the term from Kant but imbues it
with a somewhat different meaning) imposes on humanity as
a collectivity the prudential requirement of constructing a
moral memory that can be universally understood, shared,
transmitted, and defended. To do anything less would be to leave
humanity itself vulnerable to what Margalit describes as "the
effort of [the forces of radical evil] to undermine morality itself
by, among other means, rewriting the past and controlling
collective memory."

In this, as in his arguments in favor of forgiveness but
against forgetting, Margalit follows the philosopher Paul Ricoeur,
who wrote, "We must remember because remembering is a
moral duty. We owe a debt to the victims. . . . By remembering
and telling, we . . . prevent forgetfulness from killing the victims
twice." But however counterintuitive my argument may seem,
and however much one honors the moral seriousness of those
like Ricoeur, Margalit, Todorov, Yerushalmi, and Vidal-Naquet
who have advanced various, and not entirely congruent versions
of this position, what if they are wrong? What if, over the long
term, forgetfulness is inevitable, while even in the compara-

tively short term the memory of an instance of radical evil, up to and including the Shoah itself, does nothing to protect society from future instances of it?

Shortly before his death in July 2015 at the age of 106, Sir Nicholas Winton, who had traveled to Prague on the eve of the Second World War and managed to rescue 669 Jewish schoolchildren and bring them safely back to Britain, gave an interview to Stephen Sackur of the BBC. Sackur asked Winton what lessons he drew from the past. From the look of surprise on Sackur's face, he probably did not expect the answer he received. Winton was categorical. "What good does concentrating on the past do us," he demanded; "Who has ever learned anything by concentrating on the past?" Winton's question is worth the asking, as is that of the cofounder of the Annales School, the French historian Marc Bloch, who concluded his eloquent review *On Collective Memory* by commenting that Maurice Halbwachs "pushes us to reflect on the conditions of the historical development of humanity; indeed, what would this development look like without 'collective memory'?"

What if the collective memory of a nation, which Margalit himself concedes has been defined as a society that nourishes, Renan-like, a common delusion about its ancestry, is not just wildly overrated as a measure of that society's coherence, and not just ultimately futile (the message at the heart of Kipling's "Recessional"), but often actively dangerous? And what if, instead of heralding the end of meaning, a decent measure of communal forgetting is actually the sine qua non of a peaceful and decent society, while remembering is the politically, socially, and morally risky pursuit? Or, to put it somewhat differently, what if the past can provide no satisfactory meaning, no matter how generously and inclusively, as in Timothy Garton Ash's prescription, it is interpreted? In short, what if, at least in some places and on some historical occasions, the human and societal cost of the moral demand to remember is too high to be worth paying?

Almost no one believes this anymore. Marx did, when he wrote, "The social revolution of the nineteenth century cannot draw its poetry from the past, but only from the future. . . . In order to arrive at its own content, the revolution of the nineteenth century must let the dead bury their dead." And Nietzsche did, though he did not do so consistently, even when he praised "the art and power of *forgetting* and of enclosing oneself within a bounded *horizon*." But the contemporary consensus bends entirely in the opposite direction. In fairness, the most brilliant writing in defense of remembrance, and here Margalit and Todorov stand out, offers a number of caveats about how remembrance can be misused. Todorov has been especially firm in this regard, observing that "the path between the sacralization and the banalization of the past, between serving one's own self-interest and giving moral lessons to others, can seem narrow," before adding, in an echo of Galileo's "eppur si muove," "And yet it is there."

To put it kindly, such subtleties are not often in evidence in most arguments in support of collective memory as a moral and social imperative. All too many of them seem to take as their point of departure George Santayana's far too celebrated and, insofar as it was meant as a generalization, demonstrably false injunction, "Those who cannot remember the past are condemned to repeat it."⁵ This is the view that has become the conventional wisdom today, and the conviction that memory

---

5. To which Michael Herr noted in *Dispatches* the "little history joke" that "those who remember the past are condemned to repeat it too."

is a species of morality now stands as one of more unassailable pieties of our age. All of this operates at least as much under the sign of what Todorov has called moral correctness as it does under that of political correctness. To remember is to be responsible—to truth, to history, to one's faith, to one's country, to the traditions of one's own people or gender or sexuality (in this last instance what is usually meant is a group's sufferings, the history of its oppression). Anything less is an act of irresponsibility that threatens to undermine both one's community and, in our therapeutic age, oneself as well. And even to question this consensus is to disturb what Tony Judt, writing in praise of Hannah Arendt, described as "the easy peace of received opinion."

FOUR

The Victory of Memory over History

The instauration of memory as an indispensable public good, and its corollary, the damning of forgetting as a form of civic nihilism, depends on the idea, as Avishai Margalit posits it, that humanity "can be shaped into a community of memory." Margalit understands full well how difficult this will be to achieve and recognizes that it has never yet happened. He concedes, "It is hard to form effective institutions that will store such memories and diffuse them." And he points out, though without giving it the emphasis it deserves, the additional danger of what he calls "biased salience," in which events from "the so-called First World, or the technologically developed world, are likely to be more salient to us than comparable events in the Third World." Margalit does not discuss the relation between the continued dominance in the twenty-first century of the global media by Western communications companies.[1] Had he

1. The success of Al-Jazeera has not changed the basic terms of reference, the emblem of this being the fact that the network, in order to appear global

done so it would only have strengthened his argument, since the fact that, as he rightly points out, Kosovo is "better remembered" than Rwanda, is largely the result of the imbalance between the coverage of the former and of the latter.

Margalit is certainly right to worry about "a false moral superiority" being attached to atrocities that take place in Europe as opposed to those that occur elsewhere. Margalit also is right to argue that Nazi crimes "are glaring examples of what morality requires us to remember." And yet, as Tony Judt pointed out in 2008, considerable evidence already exists that in many parts of the world the Shoah is losing (if it has not already lost) what he called "its universal resonance." "Moral admonitions from Auschwitz that loom huge on the memory screens of Europeans," he observed, "are quite invisible to [many] Asians and Africans."

But even if one believes that Judt was mistaken about the particular case of the Shoah, Margalit's broader call for a shared moral memory for humankind remains problematic. Margalit himself conceded that he was "unclear in my mind as to how to go about creating such a memory." In the end, he is forced to fall back on little more than a combination of hope in the face of even the small likelihood of this hope being fulfilled—Margalit cites Romans 4:18, wherein Abraham is described as a man "who against hope believed in hope"—and his neo-Kantian resolve that *ought* implies *can*. He is hardly alone among philosophers in his confidence that, as the French philosopher Vladimir Jankélévitch once put it, "Morality always has the last word." But since elsewhere in his book Margalit admits that "we live with

---

and not "Arab" or "Third World," has hired a disproportionate number of veterans of major Western television channels as presenters on their English-language news shows.

insufficient sources to justify our ethics and morality," we might have thought this would have given him pause before he went so far in raising what the historian and poet Robert Conquest with some asperity once described as "the dragons of expectation."

This is not to say that Margalit is wrong to claim the existence of an ethics of memory. But in making the case for it, he glosses over the possibility that the reality of remembrance, and, indeed, of forgetting, which is almost of equal concern to him, might be fundamentally and ineradicably political, as Renan had understood it to be. Even when he speaks of humanity, Margalit employs a universalizing language that for the most part offers a view of the world in which there are individuals, some good, some evil, and there is the human race, as if when all were said and done there would be no need to grapple with the fact that ours is a world in which different groups of people see the world in irreconcilable or at least incommensurable ways and are almost certain to go on doing so. Even if one does not share the French social theorist Serge Latouche's anxieties about efforts to instill what he has called "the confidence trick of a bogus universality," surely in the early twenty-first century and for the foreseeable future the most pressing problem is not finding a way to instill a universal code of ethics but figuring out how to stave off the worst by arriving at John Gray's modus vivendi, in which, yes, we will have to agree to disagree on what needs to be remembered and how, and, as much if not more important, on what needs to be forgotten.

Like Todorov, whose *Abuses of Memory* has an epigraph from Jacques Le Goff enjoining his readers to "ensure that collective memory contributes to the liberation rather than the enslavement of mankind," Margalit is painfully aware that collective memory can be abused. What does not seem to command

his attention, let alone excite his skepticism, though, is the extent
to which the concept permits virtually anybody and everybody,
whatever their moral, political, or social views, to subscribe to
it. Today, fascists and multiculturalists, servants of the state and
revolutionaries committed to bringing the state to its knees,
elites and counterelites unite in paying homage to "The Duty
of Memory." We need only Google the French equivalent, *devoir
de mémoire,* to understand how protean the term has become.
The Association Devoir de Mémoire describes itself on its website as "a pageant association representing the Canadian troops
[in] World War II who worked for the liberation of Europe."
Les "Oublié-e-s" de la Mémoire is a national memorial organization that works to educate the public about the deportation
of homosexuals during the Nazi occupation of France; it campaigns in both France and elsewhere for the recognition of what
happened. Two right-wing presidents of France in succession,
Jacques Chirac and Nicolas Sarkozy, on one side of the ideological divide, and, on the other, a well-known activist group
on the hard left that calls itself Duties [plural] of Memory, have
invoked the "duty of memory" with regard to the slave trade.

The French case is extreme in the sense that, in the words
of the French historian Pierre Nora, whose pioneering research
and many books on the subject established him as the foremost
student of the role collective historical memory has played and
continues to play in French society, " 'Memory' has taken on a
meaning so broad and all-inclusive that it tends to be used
purely and simply as a substitute for 'history' and to put the
study of history in the service of memory." The takeover of history by memory is also the takeover of history by politics. The
result in practice, if not necessarily in theory, has taken us far
from Margalit's world of ethical obligations and moral minima.
Instead, we have entered a world in which the essential function

of collective memory is one of legitimizing a particular world-view and political and social agenda, and delegitimizing those of one's ideological opponents.

Renan would have loathed what Nora called the "democratization" of history, which he argued provided the ethical basis for subordinating history to collective memory. But far from undermining Renan's view, the shift Nora identified vindicates it in the sense that the creation of a given group identity is dependent on what of and how the past is remembered. What has changed, and this would indeed have profoundly worried Renan, is that whereas until the 1970s collective memory was largely a state monopoly, particularly of those elements of the state responsible for education and war—a "memorial regime of national unity," as the French political scientist Johann Michel has described it—now it is up for grabs, with ethnic, religious, and sexual minorities challenging traditional mainstream accounts and seeking to modify them if not to transform them entirely.

Does any common ground remain? The answer seems to be, "More than we might think." For no matter how bitterly the two sides differ both over *what* should be remembered and *how* this remembrance should be commemorated, they agree that not to remember would be far worse and constitute what Janké-lévitch called a "shameful amnesia." In 2008, early in his presidential term, Nicolas Sarkozy invoked the "duty of memory" when he ordered that all French schoolchildren entering their last year of primary school study the life story of one of the eleven thousand Jewish schoolchildren deported by the Nazis and murdered in the camps. His successor, François Hollande, who was then leader of the Socialist opposition, wholeheartedly endorsed Sarkozy's initiative, declaring that "any time that it is possible to transmit that which the duty of memory demands, it must be done." For their part, groups demanding that France "remember" the crimes of its colonial past and the affronts committed against groups within France itself that were excluded from the national story—even, as some campaigning associations have done, offer an apology, or reparations, whether symbolic or substantive—would endorse Hollande's formula, though the uses they would make of it are completely different.

In any case, let us assume for the sake of argument that the "memorialists," whatever their ideological inclinations, are correct in insisting, with Jankélévitch, that it is both morally shameful to forget the horrors of the past and morally uplifting to remember or, better still, to recuperate that past. Does it then follow that these are the last words that need to be said on the subject? The answer to that question has to be no—a qualified no, to be sure, but no just the same.

To be clear, I am not arguing that it is always wrong to insist on remembrance as a moral imperative. When a historical crime or tragedy has been covered up, even one that occurred long before anyone now living was born, or if the history books tell lies or a partial truth about what occurred, or even if the realities of what happened have simply become muddied, no matter whether maliciously or out of ignorance, lifting the veil about what took place is almost always something to be welcomed. The Armenian genocide is an obvious case in point; another would be the massacres perpetrated by British and French imperial forces throughout the colonial period. The same could be said about war crimes and other mass atrocities, especially if they happened in living memory. There, if a practical possibility exists not only of establishing an honest record of what was done but also of bringing the perpetrators to justice, in principle it should be done. One example of such a crime is the massacre of Muslims at Srebrenica, another the women and girls, most of them Korean and Chinese, who between 1932 and 1945 were forced by the Imperial Japanese Army into sexual slavery.

But even in such cases, things are sometimes more complicated morally than they may first appear. Most people, for example, would regard the warrant issued in 1998 by the Spanish magistrate Baltasar Garzón for the arrest of the former Chilean military dictator Augusto Pinochet as a long-overdue blow for justice. But many Chileans, including a substantial number of those who welcomed Garzón's action, also believe that had his order been issued in 1990, at the time Pinochet left office, he might have refused to relinquish power or that, had he done so, the Chilean military, which at the time was still loyal to him, would have stayed in its barracks. Under those circumstances, how can we be certain that the democratic transition would have gone forward? Assuming that the arrest might have offered at least a serious risk to that transition, would standing for the truth, or, yes, upholding the demands of justice, still have been worth it? Surely there would be nothing dishonorable in answering no to that question.

To raise this possibility is emphatically not to suggest that the answer should usually be no. To the contrary, more often than not it should be yes. When Jankélévitch denounced "shameful amnesia," for example, he was responding to those who were criticizing the French government's 1987 prosecution of Klaus Barbie for crimes against humanity—the first such case ever to be brought in France. Barbie was the former head of the Gestapo in German-occupied Lyon, and his many atrocities included personally torturing a number of prisoners to death, as well as responsibility for the deaths of thousands more, including the French Resistance leader Jean Moulin. Jankélévitch was not alone in his condemnation. It was those who opposed the trial, among other reasons on the grounds that stirring up the past could only be destructive, that Pierre Vidal-Naquet denounced in *Assassins of Memory.*

Jankélévitch and Vidal-Naquet's fears were warranted, as Adolf Hitler's own words, recorded in the transcripts later published as his "table talk," should have been enough to demonstrate. On August 22, 1939, Hitler had declared that Germany could and would exterminate the Poles "mercilessly and without compassion." The international community would not object, he said, because "Who, after all, speaks today of the annihilation of the Armenians?"[2] The accusation, fortunately not as common today as it was in the 1950s and 1960s, that Nietzsche's philosophy was one of the inspirations of Nazi ideology is a calumny. But Hitler's comment is uncomfortably close to Nietzsche's stark reminder "Whichever interpretation prevails at a given time is a function of power, not of truth."

The claim that to remember is in and of itself a moral act derives much of its force from its ambition to prove Nietzsche and Hitler wrong. The judging and execution or imprisonment of Nazi officials and concentration camp guards can never be comprehensive, and therefore cannot be put forward as a sufficient reckoning with the horror of what had occurred. In any case, even at its best, beyond assigning guilt and punishing the guilty, justice can only establish facts and at times provide the survivors and the relatives of those who did not survive with a measure of vindication and release. But as Elie Wiesel put it, "Justice without memory is incomplete justice, false and unjust.

---

2. Tzvetan Todorov has pointed out, though, that there is a rich irony in Hitler's speaking of "everyone" having forgotten an event he was himself recalling. Todorov cites a similar phrase of Stalin's about Peter the Great's murder of the Boyars.

[For to] forget would be an absolute injustice in the same way that Auschwitz was the absolute crime. To forget would be the enemy's final triumph." In this Wiesel echoes, though in universalist rather than in purely Jewish terms, the philosopher and rabbi Emil Fackenheim's injunction that if the Shoah is ever forgotten, Hitler will not only have triumphed at Auschwitz but will have won a posthumous victory as well.

What Nietzsche said about power and truth is usually understood as a cynical comment on the way in which the powerful misrepresent the truth. But although history is replete with examples that vindicate Nietzsche's claim, unless you believe that everything states do is invariably malign, in principle there is no reason why this power cannot be made to serve moral ends instead of immoral ones. Some states, notably France, have tried to enlist the law into the service of historical truth. In practice, the most important expression of this has been a series of legislative measures aimed at banning the denial or questioning in a public context of the reality of some (though not all) of the worst crimes in human history. The first of what came to be known as "memorial laws" was the *loi Gayssot* (1990), which criminalized all forms of such "revisionism" with regard to the Shoah. In 2001, a law was passed in the French parliament that recognized the reality of the Armenian genocide. In 2003 another piece of legislation, the *loi Taubira,* recognized the slave trade as a crime against humanity. And in 2005, it became an offense to deny that the Armenian genocide had taken place.[3]

There has since been some spillover from these French initiatives to the European Union as a whole. In 2007, a proposal

---

3. The *loi Gayssot* is named for the Communist deputy Jean-Claude Gayssot, the *loi Taubira* for the Socialist deputy Christiane Taubira, who would later become minister of justice during François Hollande's presidency.

in front of the European parliament was tabled that would have made punishable by a term of imprisonment an expansive array of "denialism." These included (the explanatory notes in parentheses are mine): "genocides" (plural), "war crimes of a racist character [*sic*] and crimes against humanity," "gross banalization" (that is, saying these crimes are not especially important or deserving of special status, as some French lawyers defending Nazi war criminals like Klaus Barbie had done), and even "complicity" in that banalization (no matter when the crimes in question had occurred and what political, administrative, or judicial authority had determined them to be established as historical facts).

Unsurprisingly, the consensus among professional historians has been to fiercely oppose such blanket prohibitions. They have not done this out of naïveté; after all, historians know in intimate detail the ways in which states have tried to cover up shameful episodes in their history. What most objected to was the recourse to law in the effort to combat "denialism." As Pierre Nora put it at the time the loi Taubira was passed: "Victims and orphans [of the victims] were before our eyes, and the authors of these abominations very much alive. With [the passage of the] *Loi Taubira* we reached back five or six centuries, and with the Armenians to crimes in which France played no role. What about the Vendée? . . . The Albigensians, the Cathars, the Crusades?" Nora concluded, "On the model of the *Loi Gayssot,* we are creating a system that can only constrain research and paralyze teachers."

While I share this view, it is unlikely that the series of laws Nora viewed with such dread posed a danger to historical truth of the same order of magnitude as the tendency of most governments (and probably all at one time or another) to seek to cover up not only the historical skeletons in their own closet but also those of other states, movements, or institutions with which they find themselves in sympathy. And when a government is committed to that course, the consequences for those who do try to bring what happened to light can be severe. The case of Chelsea Manning, the U.S. soldier who revealed the details of a massacre committed by her comrades in Iraq and was sentenced to thirty-five years in prison as a result, is only one of a myriad of contemporary illustrations of this.

The case of the Irish essayist Hubert Butler is illuminating in this regard. Butler was a member of the Irish Republic's Protestant minority. He was sent to an English public school and went on to attend an English university. Butler graduated in 1922 and returned to Ireland. Four years later, he left again, and for almost fifteen years traveled extensively in China, the United States, Egypt, the Soviet Union, Yugoslavia (where he spent three years), and central Europe. In 1938 and in 1939, he worked with a Quaker group in Vienna helping Jews escape post-Anschluss Austria, impelled to do so, as he would later recall, after hearing an anti-Semitic statement by the Irish parliamentarian Oliver J. Flanagan. "I was as Irish as Oliver Flanagan," Butler later recalled, "and I was determined that Jewish refugees should come to Ireland." After Vienna, Butler went to London, where he worked briefly for the British Colonial Service. But following his father's death in 1941, he returned to Ireland, moving into the family house in his native County Kilkenny, where he would live for the next fifty years until his own death in 1991 at the age of ninety.

Immediately after the end of the Second World War, Butler went back to Yugoslavia, where he tried to investigate the wartime campaign by the Nazi-installed Croatian fascist regime of Ante Pavelić to convert the almost 2.9 million Eastern Orthodox Serbs of Croatia and Bosnia-Herzegovina to Roman Catholicism, murdering many of those who would not renounce their faith. When he got back to Ireland, he gave a talk on Radio

Éireann on Yugoslavia, and, at a time when the coverage of Yugoslavia in the Irish press was focused on the victorious Tito dictatorship's persecution of religion, Butler felt honor-bound to also bring attention to what he described as "the more terrible Catholic persecution which had preceded it." In the polemics that followed, Butler was excoriated, above all for having suggested that the then archbishop of Zagreb, Cardinal Stepinac, had been complicit in the forcible conversions, which, Pavelić and Stepinac's defenders in Ireland insisted, could never have occurred in the first place, since in the words of Count O'Brien, the editor of Ireland's leading Catholic weekly, *The Standard,* "the Catholic Church has always insisted that conversion must be from the heart."

The denunciations of Butler did not stop there. Count O'Brien published a book defending Stepinac, complete with an effusive foreword by the archbishop of Dublin. Father R. S. Devane, a well-known Jesuit of the day of whom, early in his career, it was said that he "had been known to confiscate British publications from unwilling newsagents in Limerick," took up the cry that there had been no forcible conversions. For his part, James Dillon, the Irish minister of agriculture in the first interparty government of 1948–51, who later became the leader of one of Ireland's two principal parties, Fine Gael, advised a group of Irish law students to model themselves on figures such as Stepinac, Pavelić, and Cardinal Mindszenty of Hungary—all men, Dillon said, who had "gallantly defended freedom of thought and conscience." As Butler observed, "Those who knew Yugoslavia were aghast, for Pavelić . . . was the Yugoslav counterpart of Himmler."

Butler describes the furor in an extraordinary essay, "The Sub-Prefect Should Have Held His Tongue." Despite the firestorm around him, however, Butler was determined to do nothing of the sort. In 1952, he was invited to attend a public meeting in Dublin of the Foreign Affairs Association where Count O'Brien was presenting a lecture titled "Yugoslavia—the Pattern of Persecution." At the end of the talk, Butler rose to rebut what he called its "crude simplifications." As he would later write, "I had spoken only a few sentences when a stately figure rose from among the audience and walked out." The figure in question was the papal nuncio. The meeting was hastily brought to a close, and the next day, the headline in one newspaper read, "Pope's Envoy Walks Out. Government to Discuss Insult to Nuncio." As the Irish novelist John Banville puts it in his fine introduction to *The Invader Wore Slippers,* a collection of Butler's European essays, the upshot was that Butler was "forced into internal exile."

From the onset of the controversy, Butler seems to have been fully aware of the personal risks he was running. But, as he wrote, he felt he had no choice in the matter, especially because he was an Irish Protestant. Banville makes the essential point that, despite the range of his interests and the variety of his experiences, as a writer Butler was very much a localist, and cites Butler's reflection that even when his essays "appear to be about Russia or Greece or Spain or Yugoslavia, they are really about Ireland." For that reason, the controversy fell too close to home for Butler to turn away from it. For while he steadfastly insisted throughout his life that he was "an Irish Nationalist," Butler was convinced that for all their mistakes, arrogance, and other derelictions, the demonization of the Irish Protestant community in the de facto clerical state that was Éamon de Valera's Ireland was a gross falsification of history. Because of what he saw around him, Butler was unmovable. "If we agreed," he wrote, "that history should be falsified in Croatia in the interests of Catholic piety, how could we protest when our own history was similarly distorted?"

In the early 1950s, unlike in the early twenty-first century, there was still a vital distinction to be drawn between celebrity and notoriety. Butler paid dearly for his determination to set the record straight. As an Irishman of his time, he understood better than most what the cost was likely to be of tearing the scabs off such deep and as yet unhealed historical wounds. But once the controversy had subsided, Butler, who was the subtlest of writers whatever his topic, never again confronted these questions head-on. From what he did write, however, it seems evident that for him the basis of any decent society had to be a politics of truth—one in which even the most inconvenient, unwelcome, or, to use an expression much favored by genera-tions of engineers of human souls, right and left, religious and secular, "unhelpful" facts needed to be aired. As Butler put it, "If you suppress a fact because it is awkward, you will next be asked to contradict it."

This statement is that most old-fashioned of things: a noble sentiment. But as Butler himself surely would have un-derstood, the question of historical memory is a more vexed one; such binary conceptions as truth versus lie and the concealed versus the revealed get us less far than it is commonly assumed they do, and certainly nowhere near as far as we need to go. To repeat: what do we actually mean by historical remembrance and collective memory?

Here is what they cannot be: they cannot be what indi-viduals remember. As any good lawyer or police investigator will tell you, the longer the period that elapses following an accident or a crime, the less accurate and reliable the testimony of a victim or witness is likely to be. In the case of individuals, at least *some* accurate memory may remain. In the case of the historical memory of an event in history, we usually mean the collective remembrance of people who did not themselves actually live through it but rather had it passed down to them through family stories, or, likelier still in this era of acceleration, through intermediaries such as the state, above all in schools and public commemorations, or through associations, some of which commemorate versions of events that oppose or at least modify the official accounts.

When those "remembering" reach this point, can we be said to be talking about memory at all? For this is not just a flawed transmission, it is an impossible one. The verb *to remember* simply cannot be conjugated in the plural except when in reference to those who lived through what they commemorate. It is impossible to speak of a people's collective memory in the same way that we speak of individual memory: it is a metaphor meant to interpret reality and carries with it all the risks inherent in the metaphoric understanding of the world. And it is equally absurd to speak of a people's collective guilt[4] for the Shoah or for the Rwandan genocide *in the same way* that we speak of individuals' guilt for their crimes during these horrors. In her essay "Organized Guilt and Universal Responsibility," Hannah Arendt called for "a sharper dividing line between political (collective) responsibility on one side, and moral and/ or legal (personal) guilt on the other." This is the problem that lies at the heart of the effort of Arendt's friend the philosopher Karl Jaspers in his *The Question of German Guilt* (1961) to think through whether the German people could be held to have been collectively responsible for the crimes of the Nazis. Jaspers insisted on the distinction between moral guilt based on what one has done and moral guilt based on who one is, and on the necessity not to conflate the two. But today, where collective

4. As opposed to their collective responsibility, for which a strong case can indeed be made.

memory is concerned, conflating the two is precisely what we are constantly being instructed that morality and ethics require us to do. Relying as it does on highly questionable notions of collective consciousness, it is a dubious demand intellectually and, insofar as it manumits those who believe themselves to have been wronged from distinguishing between those who have actually wronged them and those who did nothing, or did not do enough, to prevent that wrong from occurring, a danger-ous one socially and politically, no matter how well intended.

FIVE

Forgiveness and Forgetting

Klaus Barbie's guilt was never really in doubt. Even his sinister, charismatic defense lawyer, Jacques Vergès, never claimed otherwise, insisting instead that the Nazis' crimes had been no different in kind either morally, or, more important, legally under the terms of the statute under which Barbie was being tried, from those committed by the European colonial empires. In *Assassins of Memory,* Pierre Vidal-Naquet ably refuted some, though not all, of Vergès's claims.[1] But for Vidal-Naquet, the greatest danger to the understanding of the Shoah came not from such Stakhanovites of moral

---

1. Vidal-Naquet himself concedes that because the Lyon court's definition of crimes against humanity, which was far broader than that of the Nuremberg Tribunal, seemed to provide the scope for Vergès to invoke the systematic torture used by the French during the Algerian War of Independence as a parallel to the crimes of the Gestapo, the advocate's argument could not be dismissed out of hand. And the distinction Vidal-Naquet makes between the French army acting in defiance of French law and Gestapo officers like Barbie acting in accordance with Nazi law seems to treat too lightly the parallels between imperialism and Nazism that Hannah Arendt pointed to in *The Origins of Totalitarianism.*

equivalence as Vergès, but rather from the "revisionists" who were determined to negate the reality of the Nazis' extermination of European Jewry. Vidal-Naquet did not underestimate what he described as "the tension, not to say [at times the] opposition" between history and memory. "History's mode of selection," he wrote, "functions differently from that of memory and forgetting." But the revisionists, by denying that the Shoah had ever happened, Vidal-Naquet argued, were attempting to sever the connections linking an anguished Jewish community that was still in mourning from its own past—in effect, trying to murder its memories.

Assuming that Yosef Yerushalmi was largely correct when, in his extraordinary *Zakhor: Jewish History and Jewish Memory*, he argued, "Only in Israel and nowhere else is the injunction to remember felt as a religious imperative to an entire people," then the affront Vidal-Naquet anatomizes is a particularly grave one. The issue of the Jewish people's in at least some way unique relation to memory is especially acute. But although in the title essay of his book Vidal-Naquet rightly emphasized the malign effectiveness, in a Jewish context, of assaulting group memory of the Shoah, he was adamant that the fundamental issue was "not one of sentiments but of truth." This claim is incontestable. Vidal-Naquet also spoke of the need for a history of Nazism's crimes to take into account "the transformations of memory." Here he seems to be referring to the attempts by the revisionists to distort and if possible annul those memories. However, there is another sense in which the transformation of memory can be understood, and it is both more puzzling and more problematic than the heroic but far more morally clear-cut struggle to which Vidal-Naquet devoted much of his life.

To put it starkly, by 2035 and probably much sooner, not a single German or non-German collaborationist perpetrator of Nazi crimes is likely to be alive since the oldest person in the world to have lived through the period will have been ten years old at the end of the Second World War. By 2045, if there are any survivors among the victims of those atrocities, they will be more than a hundred years old. When that day comes, the role of historical memory with regard to the Shoah will have a very different resonance from the one that has seemed so crucial to Vidal-Naquet and other like-minded historians and philosophers. An Emil Fackenheim or a Yosef Yerushalmi would almost certainly have disputed this, with regard to the Jewish people at any rate, on the assumption that, in Yerushalmi's words, the Jews could succeed in retaining "a commonality of values that would enable [them] to transform history into memory."[2] But it is by no means obvious that this is correct, even in the case of the Jews, this despite the fact that, in the United States at least, a 2013 Pew poll showed that an increasing number of Jews defined their Jewishness more in terms of remembering the Holocaust than of being part of a Jewish community. Surely we are obliged to ask this question: At some point in time, will not Nazi atrocities, collaboration, even the Shoah itself become what the German historian Norbert Frei somewhat regretfully categorized as, "in scholarly terms, 'plain' history"?

We have not reached this point as yet, in 2015. In Europe and North America the Shoah will probably for the foreseeable future continue to be considered what Tony Judt called a "universal reference," presented, somewhat contradictorily, both as "a singular crime, an evil never matched before or since," and as "an example and a warning." And on an individual level, in

2. Yerushalmi, who was painfully candid about his "terror of forgetting," was by no means confident this would happen. "What has long been called the crisis of historiography," he wrote in his bleak coda to *Zakhor,* "Reflections on Forgetting," "is but a reflection of the crisis of our culture, of our spiritual life."

light of the fact that the best available psychological evidence strongly suggests that the trauma survivors suffer from is passed along for two, three, or even four generations, the salience of the Shoah is unlikely to diminish a great deal for some time, if not universally then, again, at least in Europe and North America. Nonetheless, sooner or later the brute reality of the passage of time all but guarantees that a new set of difficulties will arise—one to which the mantra that, no matter how much time has elapsed, to remember a given event must always remain a defining moral imperative for any society, even assuming it is correct, does not fully respond.

A similar transition, which has in large measure been provoked by analogous actuarial realities, has already taken place in the case of the Armenian genocide. In 2015, even the youngest murderers among the Turks and Kurds who carried out the slaughter have themselves died as well. In the unlikely event that any of the Armenian survivors are still living, they are more than a hundred years old. And just as in the case of the Shoah, when the last survivors are gone who could answer questions face to face or simply roll up their sleeves to reveal the concentration camp tattoos on their arms, what will—indeed, what can—the remembrance of the Armenian genocide consist of?[3] In other words, to use the title that Leon Wieseltier gave to his fine essay on the opening of the U.S. Holocaust Museum, in the case of both of these catastrophes, what happens "After Memory"?

3. Even in this age of cyberspace, it is difficult to see how valuable initiatives like the one now being undertaken by the Illinois Holocaust Museum and Education Center, which is recording survivors' testimony and then presenting holographic representations of these interviews in which visitors ask questions and, thanks to an algorithm, survivors appear to be responding directly to them, can stand in for the survivors themselves.

There are conflicting answers to this question. On one side, there is Avishai Margalit's response, which is that the death of all those who witnessed the moral nightmare does not change by one iota the obligation of the living to protect the morality radical evil seeks to undermine. And on the other side there is Tony Judt's far more pessimistic suggestion: "Maybe all our museums and memorials and obligatory school trips today are not a sign that we are ready to *remember* but an indication that we feel we have done our penance and can now begin to let go and *forget*, leaving the stones to remember for us." Judt recalled that during a visit to Berlin's Memorial to the Murdered Jews of Europe, he saw "bored schoolchildren on an obligatory outing [playing] hide-and-seek among the stones." And he argued, "When we ransack the past for political profit—selecting the bits that can serve our purposes and recruiting history to teach opportunistic moral lessons—we get bad morality *and* bad history." To which one should add: we also get kitsch.

Even when done well, commemoration almost always skates precariously close to kitsch. One might wish that the Holocaust were an exception in this regard, and that it will always, in Leon Wieseltier's phrase, "press upon the souls of all who learn of it." But it is not, much as we might wish otherwise. This is a distinct problem, not to be confused with the fact that since 1945 the Shoah has regularly been employed to serve political agendas, the most obvious, as Judt emphasized, being to justify more or less any policy of the State of Israel with regard to its neighbors or to its Arab minority. But even when the remembrance of the Shoah is innocent of such subtexts, it has still been smothered in kitsch as Milan Kundera once defined it: all answers being "given in advance and [precluding] any questions." Again, it is understandable to hope that people will be moved by an act of collective remembrance. And it is often, though not always, right to insist that they have a moral duty to remember. Where such acts become kitsch is when people take the fact that they are moved as a reason to think better of themselves.

It is unfortunate that a prime example of the instauration of this kind of kitsch remembrance is the U.S. National Holocaust Museum itself—the largest and best-known memorial to the Shoah in the world other than the Yad Vashem Memorial Museum and Center in Israel. To be sure, much of what is in the museum is as heartbreakingly far from kitsch as it is possible to get—above all, what Wieseltier called "the objects, the stuff, the things of the persecutions and the murders," when he rightly described the Holocaust Museum as "a kind of reliquary." But these exhibits and films, photographs, and documents are bracketed by two extraordinarily kitschy pieces of set dressing. As one first enters the museum and before one has seen a single image or artifact of either Nazi atrocity or Jewish martyrdom, one must first walk by the serried battle flags of the U.S. Army divisions that liberated some of the concentration camps (there are no British or Russian standards, even though a great many of the museum's exhibits concern Bergen-Belsen, liberated by the British, and Auschwitz, liberated by the Soviets). And as one leaves the last room of the museum, the final exhibit one sees contains a series of images of David Ben-Gurion proclaiming the independence of the State of Israel, and, beyond them at the exit, a column of tan sandstone that is simply identified as having come from Jerusalem.

One can only hope that in addition to the American triumphalism and what even by the most generous of interpretations is a highly partisan pro-Israeli view of the creation of the state as the existential remediation of the Nazis' war of extermination against the Jews, the intention here was to palliate what, apart from the part of the exhibit devoted to the Danes' rescue of most of their country's Jewish population, is the pure horror of what the museum contains by beginning and ending on an uplifting note. The impulse is an understandable one. But it is also both a historical and a moral solecism that perfectly illustrates Judt's admonition that the result is both bad history and bad morality.

The current emphasis both in Israel and in the Jewish diaspora that is exemplified by the museum's last exhibit and that presents the Jewish state's moral legitimacy as inextricably bound up with the Shoah seems to me an indefensible justification of the Zionist project *in Zionist terms,* at least in the long run. It is both ahistorical, since obviously Zionist-inspired Jewish immigration to Palestine far predates the Shoah, and morally dubious, since the Palestinians bear no responsibility for what the Nazis did. As a matter of history, though not of morality, what a Zionist would be on firmer ground claiming is that at the heart of the Zionist project itself, secular and religious alike, is the conviction that the land of Israel with Jerusalem as its capital is not just the historic but the spiritual home of the Jewish people, who in all their wanderings never relinquished what the Israeli writer Yoram Kaniuk once called their mystical deed to it. In this sense, at least, it is surely fair to say that whatever the justice or injustice of this claim, without the preservation of Jewish collective memory over the centuries the establishment of the modern State of Israel would have been far more difficult. As he did so often, Yosef Yerushalmi got to the heart of the matter when he wrote, "Jewish historiography can never substitute for Jewish memory."

To say this is not to imply that Zionism is concerned only with historical continuity, whether (to the extent that the two are distinguishable) real or "invented." But it does not augur well for what the remembrance of the Shoah will become after it has passed into history in Norbert Frei's sense that the first exhibit of the museum dedicated to commemorating it is in reality little more than an ostentatious display of American nationalism and that the last is kitsch Zionist theodicy pure and simple. But unsettling and unseemly as they are, neither such American narcissism nor the Jewish communitarianism that Vidal-Naquet in his preface to *Assassins of Memory* declares he is determined to transcend tells the whole story. To the contrary, Holocaust memorials and museums are attempts to keep faith with two moral imperatives: honoring and remembering those who died and, by reminding as many people as possible of the murder of European Jewry, helping individuals and societies alike become more resistant to such evils, and perhaps even to prevent them from recurring in the present or in the future.

These matters are delicate, as they should be, and if we take such questions on we have a moral obligation to proceed with great caution. But about the argument that the memory of the Shoah is likely to have a deterrent effect—the view encapsulated in the injunction "Never Again"—there simply is no way of avoiding the conclusion that this is magical thinking, and of a fairly extreme kind. I am reminded again of Sir Nicholas Winton's remark that no one ever truly learned anything from the past. Yes, "Never Again" is a noble sentiment. But unless one subscribes to one of the cruder forms of progress narratives, be they religious or secular, there is no reason to suppose that an increase in the amount of remembrance will so transform the world that genocide will be consigned to humanity's barbarous past. This is where the contemporary heirs and assigns of Santayana go wrong: we never repeat the past, at least not in the way he was suggesting we did. To imagine otherwise is to leach both the past and the present of their specific gravity. Auschwitz did not inoculate us against East Pakistan in 1971, or East Pakistan against

Cambodia under the Khmer Rouge, or Cambodia under the Khmer Rouge against Hutu Power in Rwanda in 1994.

In contrast, establishing the historical truth about a great crime while those who committed it and those who were or at least knew its victims are alive often not only should but also can be done (as opposed to cases where doing so ought but, contra Kant, often *can't* be done). But such efforts require the investigators to think like historians, investigating the facts and letting the chips fall where they may. If politicians subsequently use the findings of Truth Commissions to their own ends, as they have done in South Africa and in Argentina, to name two of the most obvious examples, this is a price well worth paying. Yerushalmi was doubtless correct to emphasize the greater importance of memory over historiography in the Jewish tradition. But in investigating occluded truths from the past, surely it is history that must be the senior partner and memory the junior one, at least if the goal is, as it should be, to amass the facts necessary to establish an unimpeachable historical record—something that collective memory, which, as even most of its staunchest advocates concede, involves "editing" the past to further the needs of the present, rarely if ever does well.

In the aftermath of the fall of a dictatorship, assembling a reliable and comprehensive record is always important. In the case of apartheid South Africa, the Chile of General Pinochet, or the Argentina of General Leopoldo Galtieri, it was especially urgent because when they were at the height of their power these regimes had taken pains to commit their crimes in secret, just as the Nazis had. And also like the Nazis, they had attempted to cover up the remaining traces of what they had done once they realized they might be ousted from power. There need not even be a change of regime. Klaus Barbie's trial did not unveil much about the crimes the Nazis committed during their occupation of France that was not already widely known. But such was not the case when Maurice Papon finally came to trial before a French court in 1998. Papon had been secretary general for police in Bordeaux under Vichy, and had played a key role in the deportation of sixteen hundred Jews from that city to German concentration camps. After the war, however, far from being treated as the war criminal he was, Papon was seamlessly reintegrated into the French state, and during both the Fourth and the Fifth Republics he served in a series of important posts: prefect in Algeria during the Algerian War of Independence, chief of police of Paris, and finally budget minister during Valéry Giscard d'Estaing's presidency.

Papon's trial, in contrast to that of Barbie, did have some of the same morally emancipatory effect in France that the Truth and Reconciliation processes in South Africa and Latin America have had. This may seem surprising to those unversed in the history of post–World War II France, but it took decades for the truth to come out about what had happened between the country's defeat in 1940 and its liberation in 1944. Indeed, until the pathbreaking book on Vichy by the American historian Robert O. Paxton appeared in a French edition in 1973, there had been great unwillingness in France to acknowledge the fact that from a strictly legal perspective, it was Pétain in Vichy and not De Gaulle in London who had been the legitimate leader of his country. And it was not until the 1981 screening on French television of Marcel Ophuls's film *The Sorrow and the Pity*, which had been made in 1969 but banned from the airwaves for twelve years, that the consensual silence about the extent and enthusiasm of French collaboration with the Nazis began to lift. (Hara Kazuo's 1987 documentary, *The Emperor's Naked Army Marches On*, which broke with the established notion of the Japanese as the "victims" in World War II, had a somewhat similar effect in Japan.) And it lifted slowly. When Ophuls's film was first shown, French schoolchildren were still being taught that the main current in German-occupied and Vichy France alike had been the Resistance. Airing the truth provoked consternation, denial, and above all anger that such divisive facts had been allowed to come to light. The Gaullist party denounced the film as unpatriotic. At the time, many French people, in all probability a majority, agreed.[4]

The fact that their objectors' fears turned out to have been groundless has sometimes been held up by those who call for more of what the American ethicist Jeffrey Blustein has described as "doing justice to the past" as evidence that not only is getting to the truth about the past a moral imperative but that those who fear its negative effects have far less cause to do so than they suppose. In *The Moral Demands of Memory,* Blustein gives a nuanced account of the role an apology can play. When made properly, he argues, it can create new terms of reference between the "responsible party" and the "aggrieved party," with the result that "the past no longer *means* what it meant before the apology." This is a claim so sweeping it makes the Renaissance alchemists who believed they could turn base metals into gold seem almost modest by comparison, though Blustein qualifies it by saying that the longer the delay in issuing such an apology, the more the affront of the original injustice is likely to be compounded. Following the argument of Adam Nossiter's *Algeria Hotel: France, Memory, and the Second World War,* Blustein points specifically to the fact that it took fifty years, from 1945 to 1995, for a French president, Jacques Chirac, to apologize

4. An Ipsos poll conducted at the time of the Barbie trial showed that a majority of those surveyed wished it were not being held.

to French Jews on behalf of the French people, thus assuming national responsibility for their persecution. But for Blustein, however welcome, that apology failed to "repair the injustice because it [did] not address the fact that the apology was so long in coming."

As in the case of the distinction that can be drawn between the effect on Chilean democracy that indicting Pinochet at the time he relinquished power would have had and doing so eight years later had, however, delay is not always the moral solecism it is often claimed to be. The reality, however unpalatable, is that collective remembrance has not always been a salutary goad to peace and reconciliation, nor has the failure to remember, or, more precisely, in Blustein's term "properly" remember, an injustice that a particular group has suffered been toxic to their societies. To the contrary, at numerous times and in numerous places, remembrance has provided the toxic adhesive that was needed to cement old grudges and conflicting martyrologies, as it did in Northern Ireland and in the Balkans for generations, if not for centuries.

The question arises: Despite the overwhelming consensus to the contrary, does not the historical record—again contra Kant—in the world as it is and not the world as philosophers have claimed it should be and might one day become justify asking whether in some places and at some moments in history what has ensured the health of societies and individuals alike has been not their capacity for remembering but their ability to forget? What I propose is not replacing a *bien-pensant* fairy tale about memory with a *mal-pensant* cautionary tale about forgetting. Nor do I suggest that, even if I am right about the uses of such forgetting, it should take place in the immediate aftermath of a great crime or while its perpetrators are still at large. Leaving the needs of history aside, these are moments when commonsense morality and the minimal requirements of justice weigh strongly in favor of remembrance. There are certainly also times when relations between states can be improved and much bitterness removed when a state that has committed a crime against another state acknowledges its culpability. And the same is also the case when the crimes being committed are by a state against its own people.

The history of the relations between Poland and Russia is instructive in this regard. For generations, there was a bitter joke in Poland: "Who does a Pole kill first, a German or a Russian?" "A German, of course; duty before pleasure." Today, Russo-Polish relations are again strained by the Russian Federation's actions in Ukraine. Nonetheless, because in 2010 the Russian parliament finally acknowledged that Russia, not Nazi Germany, was guilty of the mass murder of twenty-two thousand Polish officers in the Katyn forest in western Russia in 1940, in another generation that joke will almost certainly make little or no sense to contemporary citizens of Poland, Germany, or Russia. To put it starkly, we should never underestimate the power of an official apology or deny that memory can be the catalyst for it.

There are at least some intimations in Maurice Halbwachs's work that he considered memory to be strongly linked to the hope for progress. It is a connection that Avishai Margalit makes explicitly in *The Ethics of Memory* when he writes, "Even remembering the gloomiest of memories is a hopeful project [because] it ultimately rejects the pessimist[ic] thought that all will be forgotten, as expressed by Ecclesiastes." Margalit is not just calling for remembrance for remembrance's sake. Quite the contrary, he believes there to be both an absolute moral obligation to remember and, at times and depending on the case, lessons to be taught and learned by doing so. Assume for the sake of argument that Margalit is right about the obligation: does this mean that he is also correct in his estimation of the enduring pedagogic value of collective memory? Tony Judt was far closer to the mark when he wrote, "The trouble with lessons, as the Gryphon observed, is that they really do lessen from day to day."

Eventually, there comes a time when the need to get to the truth should no longer be assumed to trump all other considerations. Kant thought that no right action could ever have a wrongful element. Perhaps it is because I spent fifteen years observing and writing about what for lack of a better term we call humanitarian emergencies, which are almost invariably situations in which (and this is very much a best-case scenario) even when relief groups are overwhelmingly doing good they are also doing some harm,[5] but I confess I do not see how this could ever be true. Almost as incomprehensible is the neo-Kantianism of the international human rights establishment, which refuses to entertain the possibility that when they call for justice, above all an end to impunity, the long-term consequences may prove to have had abidingly negative effects,[6] though they will sometimes concede that in the short run there might be negative as well as positive effects, particularly in war zones while fighting still rages.

---

5. Although many such groups routinely deploy the line from the Hippocratic Oath, "First do no harm," what they almost always strive for in practice is "Minimize harm as much as you can."

6. While it is exasperating and holier-than-thou, it seems more like self-promotion than an intellectual solecism when major human rights groups call for stopping a war without having any idea of how to do so, as, for instance, when Kenneth Roth, the head of Human Rights Watch, tweeted on July 5, 2015, "Want to stop flood of refugees? Curb atrocities at source: Syria, Afghanistan, Somalia, Sudan."

It is not that international human rights activists are unaware of how terrible late-twentieth- and early-twenty-first-century wars can be. The present age is one in which most hot wars are one form or another of civil or insurrectionary war within states, or, as in Iraq, to paraphrase Clausewitz, the continuation of terrorism by other means, a situation that seems to make the Geneva Conventions and the other elements of international humanitarian law, most of which were originally devised in the age of interstate war, less and less fit for their purposes. Human rights workers on the ground know this as well as or better than anyone. But the majority of them insist—whatever some may believe privately—that they must proceed on the basis that without justice there can be no lasting peace. One explanation for their absolutism in this regard is that it derives from the fact that the human rights movement is first and foremost grounded in law; its proponents have imbibed not just Kant's idealism but another element in the Kantian worldview that holds that the imperative of justice "outranks" all other moral claims.

Empirically, this is highly debatable, as the case of Bosnia illustrates. From a human rights perspective, the 1995 Dayton Peace Agreement that ended the Bosnian War was an unjust peace that let Slobodan Milošević, the principal architect of the death of Yugoslavia, along with the army and militia commanders and Serb nationalist politicians who had served him, off the hook both politically and judicially; it was only after another Balkan War, this time in Kosovo in 1999, that the great powers involved in the conflict decided to put an end to the impunity Milošević had enjoyed since Dayton. And the human rights establishment was correct: it *was* an unjust settlement. But for many of us, who, whether as aid workers or journalists, had seen the horror of the Balkan wars at firsthand, almost any peace, no matter how unfair, was infinitely preferable to the seemingly endless infliction of death, suffering, and humiliation.

Those who, with Fackenheim and Yerushalmi, believe forgetting to be a moral catastrophe, or at a minimum the half-way house toward it, often invest remembrance with the same moral authority that justice has for the international human rights movement. And the two views overlap, as when in the essay "Reflections on Forgetting," in his *Zakhor*, Yerushalmi asked whether it were possible that the "antonym of 'forgetting' is not 'remembering,' but 'justice'?" Even if he was right, however morally attractive his formulation, it does little to invalidate the empirical claim that in the world as it is, peace and justice can sometimes be inimical to each other. This reality should be cause for mourning: it certainly was for the victims of a war such as the relatives and friends of the eight thousand Bosnian men and boys massacred at Srebrenica, where the failure to secure justice for them has inflicted a moral affront in addition to all that they have already suffered.

Still, those who insist that there can be no lasting peace without justice[7] blind themselves to reality. The sad fact is that history is replete with outcomes that provided the first while denying the second. When General Pinochet stepped down in 1990, for instance, thus clearing the way for Chile's return to democracy, it was clear that justice had been not done. But the demand for democracy seemed more compelling to more Chileans who had opposed Pinochet (if not necessarily to all the families of Pinochet's victims) than did the demand for

7. As opposed to the entirely defensible claim that there can be no decent society without justice, which I often feel is what human rights activists actually mean.

justice. At the time, what appeared to be a grant of immunity to Pinochet seemed like a price worth paying. That a measure of justice was finally done eight years later when Judge Garzón handed down his indictment cannot change the earlier injustice. But put the case that Pinochet had never been indicted and arrested. In a hundred years, how many Chileans are likely to look back on the transition from dictatorship to democracy in Chile in the 1990s and conclude that impunity for Pinochet had been an intolerable price to pay for their country's freedom?

Here it may be useful to invoke Pierre Nora's distinction between the imperatives of memory and the imperatives of history, and to add to it the contingencies of politics that so often seem to hover over both. "Memory is life," Nora writes, "borne by living societies founded in its name. It remains in permanent evolution, open to the dialectic of remembering and forgetting, unconscious of its successive deformations. . . . Insofar as it is affective and magical, [it] only accommodates those facts that suit it." My imaginary Chilean of a hundred years hence would fit comfortably into Nora's rubric of memory. In contrast, that Chilean would fit far less easily into the rubric of history, which Nora defines as "the reconstruction, always problematic and incomplete, of what is no longer." For Nora, the relationship between history and memory is dialectical: "Memory instills remembrance within the sacred; history, always prosaic, releases it again."

As a complement to Nora's evocation of the sacred, I would add that collective memory often also functions as an escape and an idyll, providing a moral warrant for nostalgia—an extremely problematic emotion ethically, not least because, to reverse Freud's conclusion about mourning, deference to reality *never* gains the day. The Cuban-American writer Orlando Ricardo Menes was making a related point when he wrote,

"Idyllic memories are a jeweled noose." He knew what he was talking about: the Cuban exile community in the United States to which Menes belongs provides a textbook case of the way nostalgia and self-absorption (the other cardinal vice of the exiled and the scorned), however understandable a community's resorting to them may be, also often serve as a prophylactic against common sense, political or otherwise.

But Cuban Americans are hardly alone in their self-imposed predicament; at various points in their history, the Irish, the Jews, the Armenians, and the Tamils have been equally trapped in their own particular versions of what the writer Svetlana Boym has called "the dictatorship of nostalgia."

SIX

The Memory of Wounds and Other Safe Harbors

"It is possible that there is no other memory than the memory of wounds." If we accept Czesław Miłosz's formulation, we must acknowledge the danger that sacralizing collective remembrance is likely to lead to even graver distortions of historical reality than the use of collective memory in the service of the self-glorification of the state, or, for that matter, from the efforts rich and powerful individuals have made throughout history to assert their preeminence by ensuring they will be remembered. At least states have often been straightforward about the pragmatic political nature of the commemorative project. A good example of this, which Jacques Le Goff cited in his essay "Memory: Written and Figured," is the report on the bill in the French parliament that in 1880 reestablished the July 14 Bastille Day national holiday, invented during the Revolution but banned by Napoleon. The *rapporteur* had stated matter-of-factly that the main purpose of a celebration of this type was to remind the people "of the memories that are linked to the existing political institution," which, he asserted, "is a necessity that all governments have recognized and put into practice."

And as both Le Goff and his friend and colleague, the French classical historian Paul Veyne, have pointed out, the phenomenon of rich philanthropists, in Veyne's words, sacrificing "part of their wealth to ensure the memory of their role" dates back to Greco-Roman times. To a great extent, the practice continues largely unchanged twenty-five hundred years later, especially in the United States and Canada, where at least since the rise of private philanthropy during the Gilded Age of the late nineteenth century, an increasing number of hospital buildings and hospital centers, as well as business schools, libraries, residence halls, and other university buildings, along with theaters, concert halls, and other cultural centers, have borne the names of the philanthropists who underwrote them, just as tennis and golf stars wear the logos of their corporate sponsors on their clothes when they compete. This goes on even though philanthropists certainly know—shades once more of Shelley's "Ozymandias"—that sooner or later their names may be removed from, say, a building when it needs to be refurbished and the price the philanthropist willing to underwrite the new construction is likely to demand will be the replacement of the original donor's name with his or her own. Even here, there is a depoliticized echo of classical times, when after an emperor's death the Roman Senate often removed his name from a building or a monument that during his lifetime the senators had named after him.[1]

---

1. In 2015, for example, the billionaire philanthropist David Geffen donated $100 million to refurbish the concert space at New York's Lincoln Center then named Avery Fisher Hall, after its original benefactor, on condition that it be renamed David Geffen Hall. In accepting his offer, Lincoln Center was obliged to pay the Fisher family $15 million.

But the effects of instilling collective memory based on a sense of national or individual greatness differ significantly from those of memory anchored in a sense of personal and collective injury, whether physical, legal (discrimination), or cultural or psychological (exclusion), or in a sense of shared suffering. Indeed, while both typologies involve collective memory, the difference between the former and the latter may be summed up as that which exists between the memory of a victory and the memory of a defeat. The former may offend or annoy because of its triumphalism, in the way that British and Belgian commemorations of the hundredth anniversary of the Battle of Waterloo irked the French, or, more properly, a segment of the French political and cultural establishment, or that African American veterans of the Second World War were rightly offended at the failure of U.S. memorial celebrations to pay tribute to their role. But whether such complaints were worth taking seriously, as was the case with the black U.S. veterans, or were of no consequence, as with the Waterloo centennial, to the extent there were any at all, their harmful effects were comparatively small. In contrast, it is difficult to imagine how the Serb nationalist obsession with the Battle of Kosovo Polje in 1389 could have been more destructive to everyone affected by it, including, of course, the nationalists themselves.

Avishai Margalit confronts this problem head-on in *The Ethics of Memory.* Why, he asks, did the memory of Kosovo Polje wreak such havoc in the former Yugoslavia in the 1990s, whereas the memory of the Battle of Hastings of 1066 that sealed the Norman conquest of England has had no such harmful effects? Margalit's question is better than his answer. He seeks to rebut the claim of the American political philosopher Russell Hardin, who himself evoked the Kosovo Polje–Hastings dichotomy to buttress his own argument that "the assertion of historical memory contributes to mystification rather than explanation or understanding." But in order to do so, Margalit resorts to the claim that, historically, Hastings was a less dreadful and haunting event for the English than Kosovo Polje had been for the Serbs. According to Margalit, the former was "more a war of succession . . . [and] besides, mostly good things happened in England after the battle," while the latter had "marked the fall of a glorious Serbian independent state . . . [and] the inception of a vassal state for four hundred years under the Ottomans, an alien force with a different religion."

Margalit's historical claims are unconvincing in and of themselves. To say that mostly good things happened in England after Hastings is, to put it charitably, an extreme form of the already highly questionable Whig interpretation of British history in which the country's past is asserted to have been an inevitable progression toward ever greater liberty and constitutional government. And the Battle of Hastings, far from being comparable to, say, the peaceful ascension to the British throne of William of Orange in 1688 (the so-called Glorious Revolution), led to the virtually complete destitution of the defeated Saxon nobility by the Norman invaders so that within twenty years 95 percent of the land south of the River Tees in the north of England had passed into Norman hands. A highly romanticized, but by no means entirely inaccurate account of the tensions between Normans and Saxons long after the Conquest can be found in Sir Walter Scott's novel *Ivanhoe* and, far more dubiously, in some of the popular legends about Robin Hood that represent him as a leader of resistance against Anglo-Norman rule.

But even though Margalit's irenic rendering of British history cannot be defended, Margalit nonetheless offers, along with Todorov, the most lucid early-twenty-first-century arguments in favor of the idea that societies and the individual human beings of which they are composed have a general duty to remember but no equivalent general duty to forget. By this Margalit means that memory plays a crucial role in allowing us to understand not just where we came from but who we are. As a consequence, unless we are mystics who have chosen to withdraw from the world, we have a duty both to ourselves and to our societies to remember: "Who we are depends on our not forgetting things that happened and that are important in our lives." Perhaps if Margalit believed that it was possible to forget *voluntarily,* he would not have been so categorical. But he does not. Philip Roth's inspired phrase "Remember to forget" is for Margalit a contradiction in terms. Instead, Margalit likens the cognitive and social systems of remembrance and forgetting to the essential functional difference between the somatic and the autonomic nervous systems—the muscles controlled by the former work "on the demand" of the brain, while the latter do not. "I can voluntarily think of a white elephant," he writes, "but I cannot follow the instruction not to think of a white elephant." From this he draws the conclusion that "forgetting cannot be voluntary."

But here, whereas Margalit remarks early in *The Ethics of Memory* that he shares "Wittgenstein's belief that the first philosophical move should be to loosen the grip of metaphor," he seems trapped by the limitations of the powerful neurological metaphor that he puts forward to buttress his critique of forgetting. For while it is obviously true that an individual cannot choose to *forget* in the literal sense, it is equally true that societies cannot choose to *remember* in the literal sense. And that is because unlike individual memory, collective memory is a metaphor too, as Yerushalmi conceded when he wrote, "The 'memory of a people' is a psychological metaphor." Margalit acknowledges this when he writes, "There is nothing natural about shared memory, and nothing natural about the groups that are the natural candidates for being communities of memory. . . . They are all, in the jargon of today, social constructs." It is Margalit himself, then, and not Philip Roth who has made the fundamental error. Because if communities of memory and the collective memories they "decide" to share are social constructs—as of course they are—then in and of itself it is no more unnatural, immoral, or impossible to posit the feasibility of a socially constructed community of forgetting than one of remembrance. Neither is less artificial, or, more to the point, less imaginable than the other. This does not mean that one cannot favor remembrance over forgetting on moral grounds, but it does make specious the claim that the former is more "real" than the latter.

In his "Reflections on Forgetting," Yerushalmi describes being struck when a friend sent him a report of a *Le Monde* poll conducted at the time of the Barbie trial in which respondents were asked: "Of the following two words, 'forgetting' or 'justice,' which is the one that best characterizes your attitude toward the events of this period of the war and the Occupation?" As we have seen, this led Yerushalmi to a new formulation: Was it possible "that the journalists have stumbled across something more important than they perhaps realized . . . [and that the] antonym of 'forgetting' is not 'remembering' but 'justice'?" Margalit also seems to view forgetting as a kind of injustice, though he is more concerned that forgiveness come before forgetting than that forgetting never take place. "I maintain," he writes, "that what is needed for successful forgiveness is not forgetting the wrong done but rather overcoming the resentment that accompanies it."

Let us accept that Margalit is right when he asserts not only that this process can happen but that it has already happened in the past and will happen again.[2] But as Margalit certainly knows as well as anyone, there also have been numerous times in history when this has not happened—that is, when societies or groups within societies could not overcome their resentment, when they could not forgive—and that too will recur.[3] His schema has much to offer with regard to how societies should best respond in such cases, and, indeed, how they can prevent the resentment from fueling a new conflict while the search for an accommodation of some kind continues. To cite one example, this was the challenge facing those attempting to negotiate a peace agreement in Northern Ireland throughout the decade leading up to the Easter Sunday accords of April 1998 that finally largely brought the country's long war to a close. And Jacques Le Goff's hope that (collective) memory will aid the liberation rather than the enslavement of humanity is relevant here. But while Le Goff's sentiment is one that no sane human being could fail to wish were always the case, it too begs the question of what happens when it isn't. Are we to wait for people to come to their senses? If so, we may be in for a very long wait indeed. Or is it possible that this is where forgetting without the preamble of forgiveness or the promise of justice has a value that even thinkers as brilliant as Le Goff, Margalit, Todorov, and Yerushalmi have not been able to bring themselves to grant?

2. To some extent, though not as greatly as the received wisdom outside the country would lead one to believe since it had and still has many opponents, this can be said to have occurred in the case of the Truth and Reconciliation Commission in South Africa.

3. See, for example, the fury with which Bosnian crowds greeted the arrival of the Serbian prime minister, Aleksandar Vučić, at the twentieth-anniversary ceremonies in 2015 marking the Srebrenica massacre.

I do not claim that forgetting would be an appropriate response in cases where justice or forgiveness (or both) are a realistic alternative, as in many cases, including some grave and seemingly intractable ones, they will be. But the ultimate metric here should not be the ideal but the probable, or at least the feasible. Bismarck's celebrated remark that no one should look too closely at the making of sausages or laws surely applies even more forcefully to peace settlements. When it is possible, by all means let societies remember, provided of course—and this is a very big caveat indeed, and one those convinced that remembrance is a moral imperative consistently underestimate—remembering does not engender further horrors. But when it is not possible, then, to paraphrase the slogan of the anti–Vietnam War movement of the late 1960s, it may be time to give forgetting a chance, which is another way of saying that it is time to give politics a chance and idealism a rest.

And idealism it most emphatically is. Take, for example, Todorov's observation that for historical remembrance to have enduring value and be of enduring help to the societies that undertake it, it must lead to "a [generalizable] principle of justice, a political ideal, or a moral rule [that must be] legitimate in and of themselves [*sic*] and not because they derive from a memory that is dear to us." On the basis of what historical evidence, or, indeed, of any principle other than hope, should we conclude that this is where the exercise of collective memory is likely to lead us? And since, in contrast, we know that historically memory has been and continues to be toxic in many parts of the world, why put our ethical trust in it, no matter how morally desirable such an outcome might prove to be?

We do, after all, already understand the risks. Like Margalit, Miłosz was being metaphorical when he mused about whether human beings had any memory other than the memory of wounds. But there have certainly been periods in the history of every nation, and probably every community, in which making such a claim has required no poetic license. Again, the case of Northern Ireland stands out, since there, until the late 1990s, as one Ulster poet put it, the country got "martyrs when it needed men." Those were the days when remembrance was hatred's forge and forgiveness was not on offer. Is it not, then, at least worth considering, if only as a thought experiment, whether it might have been better for everyone in the six counties of Northern Ireland if they had found a way to forget the wrongs of the past, whether real or imagined, and whether accurately or inaccurately "remembered"?

Like any counterfactual, the question is one that can have no definitive answer. But what we know all too well is the damage collective memory can do. The Irish writer and politician Conor Cruise O'Brien once observed of a particularly dark and despair-inducing period of the conflict in Northern Ireland that during the secret negotiations in which, as a member of Garet Fitzgerald's government in Dublin, he had been involved, just as it seemed as if Republicans and Unionists might finally, painstakingly be coming close to an agreement, a representative at the talks from one of the two sides would remember one of great militant songs—the IRA's "Rising of the Moon" or the Ulster Volunteer Force's "Sash My Father Wore"—and whatever hope had existed would soon vanish. Cruise O'Brien was much given to embellishment, but in this instance he didn't need to. Those who may be tempted to doubt the potency of those songs might recall that "the rising of the moon" were the last five words of the final entry in the prison diary kept by the Provisional IRA leader Bobby Sands before he died on the sixty-sixth day of the hunger strike he had organized and led among the Republican prisoners in the Long Kesh (Maze) prison in County Down, Northern Ireland, in 1981. "They won't break me," Sands had written of the prison authorities, "because the desire for freedom, and for the freedom of the Irish people, is in my heart. The day will dawn when all the people of Ireland will have the desire for freedom to show. It is then we'll see the rising of the moon."

There are also echoes in Sands's diaries of *The King's Threshold,* a play about a hunger striker set in the mythical past that Yeats had written in 1904, but which, as Sands surely knew, Yeats had rewritten in 1920 in the aftermath of the death on hunger strike of the imprisoned Sinn Féin lord mayor of Cork, Terence MacSwiney, himself a playwright. Sands's act also seemed born of the same conviction that had led Patrick Pearse to confidently insist that even if the Easter Rising ended in failure, and he himself was killed by the British (he was), his and his comrades' deaths would be a "blood sacrifice" that would stir the whole Irish people and lead to their rising up and finally seizing their independence. Of Sands's hunger strike and eventual death, Seamus Heaney, Ireland's greatest poet since Yeats, himself originally from County Derry in Northern Ireland, subsequently wrote: "I was highly aware of the propaganda aspect of the hunger strike and cautious about being enlisted. There was realpolitik at work; but at the same time, you knew you were witnessing something like a sacred drama."

As Heaney knew well, sacred drama is the antithesis of any decent politics. For once the sacred has been invoked, there can be no compromise with one's adversaries, only their unconditional surrender. To the extent that this can still be called politics, it is a politics of totalitarianism. Yeats might write in his poem "September 1913," "Romantic Ireland's dead and gone; it's with O'Leary in the grave," but, in reality, as Yeats would realize in the aftermath of the Easter Rising and sum up in another poem, "Easter, 1916," with the words "a terrible beauty is born," romantic Ireland survived the Fenian John O'Leary, financial officer of the Irish Republican Brotherhood and editor of *The Irish People,* as it would survive Pearse and Easter Sunday, 1916, and MacSwiney, and Sands too. It was only the deed of the very different Easter Sunday, in 1998, that finally put romantic Ireland in its grave. That Ireland had lived and battled in poetry, whereas whatever else has gone wrong in the Ireland of the twenty-first century, the continuation of peace in the North amply demonstrates the truth of a former governor of New York State, Mario Cuomo, who said that one campaigns in poetry but governs in prose.

Poetry, which is among other things the native language of myth, facilitates long memories, while prose, at least in the Cuomo sense, helps shorten them. For as John Kenneth Galbraith admonished us, and as anyone with direct experience of practical politics knows, "Nothing is so admirable in politics as a short memory." Of course, myths, like the proverbial wires, can become crossed, allowing the legends of the distant past and the ideological needs of the present to blur into each other. Take as an example "The Dying Cúchulainn," the statue of the hero of the Irish medieval epic the *Táin Bó Cúailnge,* which stands inside the General Post Office in Dublin. The statue was made in 1911 by the Irish sculptor Oliver Sheppard, a leading figure in the Celtic Revival and an ardent nationalist. But it is there not as a tribute to ancient Ireland; it was installed in 1935 at Éamon de Valera's personal request as a memorial to the Easter Rising. Samuel Beckett treats these contradictions venomously in his novel *Murphy,* published only three years later, in which the character Neary says that he wanted to "engage with the arse of the statue of Cúchulainn, the ancient Irish hero, patron saint of pure ignorance and crass violence," by banging his head against it.

The current commonplace condemnation of contemporary life holds that because of a surfeit of technological stimulation we have shorter and shorter attention spans—but if true this has done nothing to shorten our collective memories of grievance. Whether the United States or France was the first out of the gate in this is an open question, but in the early twenty-first century there are few democratic societies that are not embroiled in their own memory wars, which have become arenas for competing, or, at the very least, for competing matyrologies. The American sociologist Jeffrey Olick has described the shift from earlier forms of official commemoration as one in which governments now "commemorate failures as well as triumphs," while "social movements and other identity groups turn to 'repressed' histories as sources of their cohesion and as justification for their programs." For Olick, Max Weber's idea of a new "theodicy of disprivilege" lies at the heart of the shift.

Where remembrance is concerned, despite impassioned assertions that truths previously concealed have been brought out into the open and need to be acknowledged, the question of historical accuracy rarely seems as crucial as does the group solidarity such remembrance is meant to engender. That this politics is anchored not just in ressentiment—the point, following Nietzsche, the philosopher Max Scheler, and Weber, that Olick emphasizes—but in radical subjectivity should come as no surprise. Moreover, it is a psychological truism that an individual's effort to recover his or her own memories, whether readily available or repressed, when done properly and seriously in a therapeutic context (Freud's *Durcharbeiten*) can be healing. Unfortunately, this has led to the psychological pop-culture commonplace that to be able to remember a traumatic experience is the necessary first step in coming to terms with it. And the same is now thought to be the case with the collective memories of social groups. This is what my late father, Philip Rieff, meant when he wrote of "the triumph of the therapeutic."

A shrewd defense of the therapeutic view has been offered by the American psychiatrist Janet Baird, who has argued that both individuals' traumatic memories and the collective historical memories of groups, for all the obvious differences in the ways these are formed, retained, and transmitted, "retain the quality of 'now,' rather than receding into the subjective past." Baird adds that where collective historical memory is concerned, social stress seems to awaken and activate "the historical memory in [such] a way that the protagonists of the past become resurrected in the 'now.'" Although what Baird describes is undoubtedly true clinically, what may be constructive for a therapist treating a patient's individual trauma could be highly dangerous politically when nations, peoples, or social groups act on their collective traumas. In this sense, to extend the psychotherapeutic metaphor, they are not treated, they self-medicate. Part of the reason for this is that while individuals' memories are often distorted (and in extreme cases, partly invented or even false), they are undeniably real in the sense that they derive from actual lived experience. In contrast, once the transmission of collective memories continues for more than three or four generations, it can no longer be called memory *other than* metaphorically. To use two storied examples, Irish men and women today do not "remember" the Great Famine of 1847, nor does an observant Jew praying in the synagogue "remember" Jerusalem.

Even far more benign examples of this are no less paradoxical. "Je me souviens" (I remember), the official motto of Québec, is one such case. The phrase was the coinage of the

architect Eugène-Étienne Taché, the son of a former prime minister of United Canada and one of the architects of Canada's
Confederation of 1867, which is to say of its birth as a modern
nation. Taché had been commissioned to design Québec's new
parliament building, and he appears to have decided, completely on his own, to add "je me souviens" to the coat of arms
granted to the province by the British crown in 1868. Although
some mid-twentieth-century Québec nationalists claimed that
Taché had had a separatist meaning in mind, there is no convincing evidence for this, as there is for the watchword "nôtre maître
le passé" (our master the past), which was an avowedly separatist rallying cry when it was coined in 1936 by Father Lionel Groulx,
one of the founders of modern Québecois nationalism.

Examples like Taché's are more the exception than the rule,
as the history of Québec after the so-called Quiet Revolution of
the 1960s amply demonstrates. The Quiet Revolution put an
end to the mixture of opportunism and clerical conservatism
that had marked the politics of the province during the long
premiership of Maurice Duplessis, which was, in significant
ways, as close as North America has come to a homegrown
Franco- or Salazar-style corporatism. It is true that Québecois
nationalism in the post-Duplessis era for the most part followed
the more conventional pattern, in which the invocation of collective historical memory is used to accentuate differences
rather than, as Taché seems to have attempted to do, to bridge
them. But the irony is that Québecois nationalism after 1965
emphasized Québec's distinctness while rupturing much of what
linked the province's present with much (some would even say
most) of its historical past. Where Québec had traditionally been
politically conservative, the new nationalist intellectuals identified themselves overwhelmingly with the left; and where Québec
had been religious, in the main, they were nonbelievers. In short,

the claim that Québec had always been a distinct society and should have become and one day would be an independent country coexisted with the repudiation of nearly everything, apart from the French language, that historically has made French Canada unique.

And yet contemporary Québec is as obsessed with commemorations of its past as the rest of the world, though the province's collective memory is now being rewritten, however grudgingly, to include what in Canada are called the First Peoples, and to focus specifically on the struggles of the ruled, rather than the rulers, and above all on women. But while the content of the debate about what should be remembered varies from country to country, the general pattern remains largely the same. The paradox is that while what Pierre Nora has rightly called the memory industry has expanded to the point that it has begun to seem like a demonstration of the second law of thermodynamics, with the appetite and quest for memories becoming ever more dispersed with time, schoolchildren in virtually all developed countries know less and less about contemporary politics, world geography, or history. And what little history they do know is not history in the proper sense of the term but remembrance. The danger should be obvious: whatever the pitfalls of history in the traditional sense, it is not narcissistic, which is another way of saying it is genuinely concerned with the past, fully taking on board the understanding that the English novelist L. P. Hartley encapsulated in the first line of *The Go-Between* (1953): "The past is a foreign country: they do things differently there." In contrast, remembrance is about self-love, and self-recognition, which means more often than not that it is little more than the present in drag.

"What is the Ninth Symphony," Karl Kraus asked, "compared to a pop tune played by a hurdy-gurdy and a memory?"

That is remembrance in a nutshell. At best, it is a consolation or an ego boost, while at worst it is a wallowing, no matter whether in past triumphs or past injuries and traumas. In contrast, history is hard, and the better the history, the more demanding and outward-looking it is. Never mind the Ninth Symphony: think Berg or Schnittke. Instantly gratifying (even if the form that gratification takes is anger, bitterness, or ressentiment),[4] the overvaluing of collective memory and the undervaluing of history is a perfect fit with the spirit of an age that is itself dominated by instant gratification. Add what the Australian writer Robert Hughes called "the culture of complaint" to a self-absorption that is one of the constitutive elements of Guy Debord's "society of the spectacle" in multicultural drag ("all that was once directly lived has become mere representation" was how Debord formulated it). On the other side of the ideological divide, throw in the old simplifications of nationalism, which, as Ernest Gellner pointed out in the 1970s, had always been opportunistically selective in what it chose to pay obeisance to, and all the sentimentality, complacency, and kitsch nostalgia that goes with it. The result? The world as pop song—and one that is more akin to the Latvian entry in the Eurovision contest than to Leonard Cohen's verities. If the memories are not actually there—and not to belabor the obvious, in the literal sense at least, they never are—teach the myth.

4. And even ressentiment is a complicated business. Jeffrey Olick, who sees this clearly, offers this insight from the radical American political theorist Wendy Brown: "Identity politics may be partly configured by a peculiarly shaped and peculiarly disguised form of class resentment that is displaced onto discourses of injustice other than class, but a resentment, like all resentments, that retains the real or imagined holdings of its reviled subject as objects of desire."

Is much of this harmless? Of course it is. But it is dangerous enough of the time, especially for peoples who, for a wide variety of historical, religious, and cultural reasons, are highly prone or at least vulnerable to self-mythologization. And we could legitimately go farther and assert that the world would be a better place if, instead of being convinced that collective memory (rightly understood, to be sure, as Margalit and Todorov would correctly insist) should be a moral imperative for us, we instead chose to forget. The last thing I want to do is replace one hypercategorical prescription with its opposite, let alone issue a jeremiad on the order of Yerushalmi's when he insisted that "in the world in which we live it is no longer merely a question of the decay of collective memory and the declining consciousness of the past, but of the aggressive rape of whatever memory remains." What can be demonstrated is the considerable extent to which many of the arguments for collective memory are in their essence profoundly anti- or at least post-political in orientation in much the way the human rights movement's arguments are. To put this in the form of two questions: If humankind is or at least can become, as Margalit would have it, a moral community, what are that community's politics? and If that community is above or outside politics, can it be a community worthy of the name?

Given that the human rights project shares with the duty of memory project the same law-based view of morality, these parallels should come as no surprise. In addition, both worldviews are absolutist, whereas the essence of democratic politics is compromise—that most effective of prophylactics against fanaticism. And even though everything will be eventually forgotten in the fullness of geological time, the conceit of collective memory is that in theory at least it can be renewed forever. Such renewal, far from ensuring justice, is a formula for unending grievance and vendetta.

SEVEN

Amor Fati

W ith the possible exception of the Jews, for whom questions of law, tradition, memory, and custom are notoriously difficult to disentangle, collective historical memory is no respecter of the past. Indeed, historically, most of the claims to continuity that are made for it are at best partly specious and often utterly so. This is not simply a matter of inaccuracy, willful or otherwise, of the type one encounters in the many contemporary television miniseries that attempt to re-create a past historical era—Showtime's *The Tudors,* say, or HBO's *Rome,* about the latter of which the classicist Mary Beard remarked that for her the great pleasure of watching it was seeing how many historical howlers could be crammed into a given episode. Such entertainments rarely if ever challenge the conventional order, and usually reflect it—think of the Hollywood films of the 1930s such as *Lives of a Bengal Lancer* and *Gunga Din,* whose hymns to colonialism Bertolt Brecht skewered so mordantly in the diaries he kept during his Los Angeles exile. In contrast, when states, political parties, and social groups appeal to collective historical memory, their motives are far from trivial.

Until well into the second half of the twentieth century, the goal of such appeals was almost invariably to foster national unity, along the same lines that Renan the historian had anatomized and Renan the nationalist had prescribed. It would be comforting to believe that damnable regimes have been more given to this practice than decent ones, which may help account for the fact that many discussions, including Todorov's and Margalit's, that attempt to validate the concept of collective memory but frankly acknowledge how often it is misused,[1] highlight Hitler's and Stalin's manipulations of the past, as in the case of Stalin's attempts to mobilize the Russian people to resist the German invasion by appealing to the memory of the medieval prince of Novgorod, Alexander Nevsky, who had repelled a previous German invasion when he defeated the Teutonic Knights at the Battle of the Ice in 1242. But the reality is that such efforts to mobilize and manipulate collective memory or manufacture it have been made by regimes and political parties of virtually every type.

There have even been times when rival political movements have vied for "ownership" of a particular historical figure who is thought to incarnate the nation. A case in point was Joan of Arc in nineteenth-century France. Between 1841, when a biography of her appeared written by the influential historian Jules Michelet, and the early twentieth century, the left and the

---

1. For Margalit, "The distinction needed . . . is between the illusion *of a* collective memory and [the] illusions *within* collective memory," while Todorov argues that one way to distinguish between its proper and improper use is whether "the actions that have been claimed to be based on it have been for the better or the worse." My own view, though, is that this criterion doesn't get Todorov nearly as far as he seems to think in establishing a viable set of criteria for making the correct choice.

right in France both claimed her as their symbol even though their portraits of the Maid of Orleans were incompatible. For the right, she was seen as the emblem of France's determination to repel foreign invaders, while for the largely anticlerical French left—and in this they were faithful to the portrait the militant anticlerical Michelet had presented of her—she was a victim of the church that had condemned her to be burnt at the stake. Once the Catholic Church beatified her in 1909 (she was then canonized in 1920), the left could no longer credibly claim her as one of their own. Yet the "memory" of Joan of Arc continued to be contested; it became a rallying point for the right, first for the extreme conservative Catholic movement, the Action française, and the Vichy government during the Second World War over which the movement exerted considerable influence, then, beginning in the late 1980s, when its leader Jean-Marie Le Pen made his first significant electoral breakthrough, for the French ultra-right party, the Front National, which commemorates Joan of Arc every May 1, not coincidentally the date of the left's most important annual holiday.

Presumably not only Tzvetan Todorov and Avishai Margalit but almost anyone who was reasonably literate historically would view skeptically the French right's manipulation of the figure of Joan of Arc. That effort to inculcate a "collective memory" to suggest that just as she incarnated France's struggle against the English foreign invaders of her time, so too does today's Front National, this time against Muslims and other immigrants that the party wishes to persuade the French people are the invaders of today, represent a gross distortion of history. Yet typologically the right's manipulation of Joan of Arc is no different from and no more inaccurate than the determined efforts of the impeccably social democratic Scottish National Party to appropriate the figure of William Wallace, the late-twelfth-century nobleman who was an early leader of medieval Scotland's wars of independence, for its own ideological and electoral ends.

If anything, the William Wallace that the SNP held out as a model for emulation for Scottish voters bears even less resemblance to the historical figure than does the Joan of Arc touted by the Front National. We probably have Hollywood to thank for this: the SNP shamelessly capitalized on Mel Gibson's preposterous biopic of Wallace, *Braveheart*, using the launch of the film in Scotland in 1995 to jump-start a massive recruitment drive for the party. Volunteers handed out leaflets to filmgoers as they left cinemas all over Scotland that read in part: "You've seen the movie—Now face the reality. . . . Today, it's not just bravehearts who choose independence, it's also wise heads." The juxtaposition was patently absurd, and yet the SNP's then vice president, Paul Scott, seemed to have no problem drafting into his party's cause the figure of a Scottish minor nobleman about whom, apart from his military campaign of 1297–98 and the ghastly details of his public execution by the English in 1305, virtually nothing is known. "In modern terms," Scott told an interviewer, "the desires of civic nationalism are exactly the same [as those of Wallace]."

There is no *inherent* difference between the use the Front National has made of Joan of Arc and that which the SNP has made of William Wallace. Yet given the contrast between the furious response to the former and the comparatively relaxed reception of the latter, one would be hard-pressed not to conclude that the objection is not to the manipulation of history but to the fact that it is the Front National doing the manipulating. As the old psychoanalytic joke would have it, "When the right person does the wrong thing, it's right; when the wrong person does the right thing, it's wrong." To be sure, at some point in their lives, almost all adults have had to confront the contingency of their convictions. But it hardly seems intellectually credible to claim that the Front National's manipulation of Joan of Arc is an abuse of collective memory while the SNP's of William Wallace is not. And one wonders whether, had the left's equally historically unsustainable claims regarding Joan of Arc prevailed in twentieth-century France, the same bienpensant severities would have been brought to bear on them.

No one who has written about collective memory has been more alert to the dangers of its abuse than Tzvetan Todorov. In 2010, for example, he returned from a trip to Argentina, where he had visited the sites commemorating the victims of the military dictatorship, including the former Navy Mechanics School in Buenos Aires—the so-called ESMA, where hundreds were tortured to death—and wrote a highly critical account of them in a column in the Spanish newspaper *El País*. "Memory," he wrote, "is subjective . . . which is why it can be used by a [particular] group as a means of gaining or reinforcing its political position." And yet Todorov has continued to insist that, while "a society needs history, not just memory," when done properly historical remembrance provides exemplary instances of more general categories, thus serving "as a model for understanding new situations involving different [historical] actors." And for him, this is at least "potentially liberating." Todorov freely concedes that "not every lesson is a good one" (to this extent, at least, echoing Margalit's vision of humanity as potentially an ethical community of memory), but he nonetheless insists that each can be evaluated on its merits "with the help of universal, rational criteria that sustain [genuine] human dialogue."

But is he right to believe this, or is he instead imputing to human beings a far greater degree both of rationality and of solidarity than we as a species possess? To insist on the point is not the same as claiming that human beings are too irrational and self-interested to learn from the past, or are incapable of applying what they have learned (and not in the reductive, Santayana-like sense, with which Todorov has never sympathized). Rather, it is to say that, contra Margalit, to ask whether collective memory exists is, in an essential sense, to ask the wrong question. Of course collective memory exists, *but only metaphorically,* which makes it subject to numerous distortions that should put the claims for its importance morally and ethically under severe strain. In his lovely book on metaphors in literature, Denis Donoghue writes, "We normally—and justly—speak of metaphor as an irruption of desire, specifically the desire to transform life by reinterpreting it, giving it a different story. . . . It expresses one's desire to be free, and to replace the given world by an imagined world of one's devising."

Is the case of history so far removed from that of literature as to be irrelevant to it? That hardly seems likely. No matter what the arena of human consciousness and thought, to apply in the name of the duty to remember an essentially metaphoric understanding of the past to the present seems far more likely to elicit unreason than reason, if on no other basis than that, in Leon Wieseltier's stark phrase, "The mind cannot do without the imagination, but the imagination can do without the mind."

If this is right, then the contradictions inherent in any definition of collective memory and not, as Ricoeur, Margalit, Todorov, and others have argued, its abuse are what make it difficult for human beings to avoid falling for or indeed propagating such historical travesties as the Front National's adoption of Joan of Arc or the Scottish National Party's of William Wallace. It is true that the metaphoric essence of collective memory does indeed free it, and allows it, as in Donoghue's sketch of it in the context of literature, to replace the given world with an imagined world of one's own devising. But it is the freedom of the permanent adolescent. And as is the case with many adolescents, remembrance too often proceeds as if gravitationally drawn to suffering, conflict, and sacrifice.

Renan saw all this clearly, and unlike the partisans of collective memory of the early twenty-first century, he viewed its emphasis on suffering as its essence rather than as a distortion or abuse of that essence: "More valuable than common customs posts and frontiers conforming to strategic ideas is the fact of sharing, in the past, a glorious heritage and regrets, and of having, in the future [a shared] program to put into effect, or the fact of having suffered, enjoyed, and hoped together. These are the kinds of things that can be understood in spite of differences of race and language. I spoke just now of 'having suffered together' and, indeed, suffering in common unites more than joy does. Where national memories are concerned, griefs are of more value than triumphs, for they impose duties and require a common effort."

From the vantage point of 2015, in an era when the grand narrative of the state has been or is in the process of being challenged, overhauled, and in some cases replaced entirely by often competing agendas of those mistreated, oppressed, and excluded by states and by dominant classes and races, what needs to be added is that these agendas too are not just strengthened by grief, as Renan understood, but sustained by the sense of traumatized victimhood on the part of both the individuals and the collectivities concerned. Most of the time, this is harmless. But not all of the time, and those are the instances when it needs to be kept in mind that there are few phenomena more uncontrollable socially and, hence, more dangerous politically than a people or a social group that believes itself to be a victim. This was what Auden was talking about in "September 1, 1939," when he pointed to "What all schoolchildren learn/Those to whom evil is done/Do evil in return."

One proof of this can be found in the fact that in the minds of their perpetrators, virtually every great crime of the twentieth century has been committed in an atmosphere of fear and with the justification of self-defense, whether reactive or preemptive, that is to say, of "us or them." The Turks thought the Armenians were a Russian fifth column; Stalin thought the Kulaks were subverting his program of agricultural collectivization on which the future of the Russian food supply depended; and the Nazis conceived of the Jews as being the moral equivalent of a lethal microbe and of having been responsible for Germany's defeat in the First World War. Despite all the promises of "Never Again" put forward in the wake of the Seond World War, in the postwar world, existential fears have driven other groups to commit mass murder in the name of self-preservation, the most terrible of which in terms of the proportion of the population that was killed was the Rwandan genocide.

If faced squarely, what these events and the motivations behind them should serve to refute is the belief that sometime in the twentieth century humanity turned an existential corner.[2] No matter how many ceremonies of commemoration we hold, no matter how many museums to the Shoah or the Great Irish Famine we build, no matter how many laws we pass along the lines of the French parliament's criminalization of the denial of the Armenian genocide, and no matter how radically we revise the school curricula in countries that grew rich off the

---

2. This view, which is demonstrably utopian, now also informs the mainstream relief and development world, where the consensus view is that for the first time in history it is not only possible but likely that by the middle of the twenty-first century extreme poverty and hunger will have all but disappeared.

slave trade in order to acknowledge its horrors, we are bound to fall short of the millenarian goals that we delude ourselves are now within our reach. However seductive the thought might be, to imagine otherwise is not going to help us remember "better" and more usefully in an ethical or social sense. Despite Todorov's injunction that it is possible to "make use of the lessons of past injustices to fight against those taking place in the present," the effect in at least some extreme situations is more likely to be to de-historicize these events, thus leaching them of their specificity. In Rwanda after the genocide, a Père Blanc who had lived through it was asked by a journalist whether witnessing it had not caused him to lose his faith in God. His immediate reply was to explain with great conviction why it had not. But then, after a short pause, he added almost matter-of-factly that it *had* destroyed forever his faith in human beings. "The devil is an optimist," Karl Kraus wrote, "if he thinks he can make people meaner."

I am not prescribing moral Alzheimer's here. Self-evidently, to be wholly without memory would be to be without a world. Nor am I arguing against the determination for a group to memorialize its dead or demand acknowledgment of its sufferings from those who inflicted them or who stood by and did nothing to prevent it. That would be as morally obtuse as demanding of traumatized individuals or family that they forget their loved ones or, in the case of physical abuse or deep psychic wound, to go on covering up what went on in the past behind closed doors. To do so would be to counsel a species of moral and psychological self-mutilation of tragic proportions. On the other hand, too much forgetting is hardly the only risk. There is also too much remembering, and in the early twenty-first century, when people throughout the world but in the Global North in particular, are, in Todorov's words, "obsessed by a new cult, that of memory," despite Yerushalmi's impassioned arguments to the contrary, the latter seems to have become a far greater risk than the former.

Hyperthymesia is a rare medical condition that has been defined as being marked by "unusual autobiographical remembering." The medical journal *Neurocase: The Neural Basis of Cognition* identifies its two main characteristics: first that a person spends "an abnormally large amount of time thinking about his or her personal past," and second that the person "has an extraordinary capacity to recall specific events from [his or her] personal past." It is similar, though not identical, to a case documented by the mid-twentieth-century Russian neurologist Aleksandr R. Luria in his *The Mind of the Mnemonist* of a man who could forget only by an act of will. Luria described this as the inability to engage in what is sometimes called "ordinary forgetting."

If we are at all skeptical about the contemporary elevation of remembrance and deprecation of forgetting, these can come to seem like nothing so much as hyperthymesia writ large. But even many people who would not go that far would probably agree that the cult of remembrance has become something of a fetish. In his magisterial final work, *Memory, History, Forgetting*, Paul Ricoeur argued that there could be no art of forgetting in the way that, since the Rosicrucians at least, there has been understood to be an art of memory. For Ricoeur, as for Margalit, what needed to be cultivated was not forgetting but forgiving. And yet even Ricoeur seems to have worried about the contemporary obsession with memory.

He was right to do so. For remembrance, however important a role it may and often does play in the life of groups, and whatever moral and ethical demands it not only responds to but often can fulfill, carries with it political and social risks that at times also have an existential character. This can be serious during wars or social and political crises, particularly when these are intercommunal or religiously inspired. In such situations, the danger is not Yerushalmi's "terror of forgetting" but rather the terror of remembering too well, too vividly.

Suppose, for the sake of argument, that Yerushalmi was correct, and that forgetting destroys not just the link with the past in the obvious formal sense but also the commonality of values that should link the living with their ancestors and their own descendants with them. Even this by no means rules out the possibility that the price of remembering, at least in certain political circumstances and at certain social and historical conjunctures, might still be too high. These are the cases, small in number, no doubt, but high in the potential for human suffering, in which it is possible that whereas forgetting does an injustice to the past, remembering does an injustice to the present. On such occasions, when collective memory condemns communities to feel the pain of their historical wounds and the bitterness of their historical grievances—and all communities have such wounds, whether at a given point in history they are oppressors or the oppressed[3]—it is not the duty to remember but a duty to forget that should be honored. And despite the eloquent arguments Ricoeur deployed against such a parallelism, if there can be a will to remember, why, if only in extremis, can there not also be a will to forget?

In these situations, at least, is it possible to state with confidence which is worse, remembering or forgetting? There can be no categorical answer. If the prospect exists of "curing

3. If the Rwandan genocide and its aftermath should have taught us anything, it is how quickly such roles can flip and how easily yesterday's victimizers become today's victims.

war," as Einstein put it in 1931 in his celebrated exchange of letters with Freud, then Margalit's championing of forgiveness without forgetting might itself be sufficient. But as Freud said in his answer to Einstein, "There is no likelihood of our being able to suppress humanity's aggressive tendencies." And if Freud was right, then it is at least possible that forgetting, for all the sacrifices it imposes (and, to be clear, these can be terrible indeed), may be the only safe response—and as such should be a cause for a measure of relief, rather than consternation. There are many historical examples of such forgetting taking place far sooner than might reasonably have been expected. As an illustration, when General De Gaulle had his historic change of heart and decided that France would have to accede to Algerian independence, one of his advisers is said to have protested, exclaiming, "So much blood has been shed." To which De Gaulle answered, "Nothing dries quicker than blood"—a reply that exemplifies Nietzsche's idea that what he called "active forgetting" is an important attribute of a man of power.

To put the dilemma even more bluntly, remembrance may be the ally of justice, but, despite the conventional wisdom of the human rights movement, it is no reliable friend to peace, whereas forgetting can and at times has played such a role. An example of this is the so-called *Pacto del olvido* (Pact of Forgetting) between the right and the left that, while never formalized, was essential to the political settlement that restored democracy in Spain in the 1970s after Franco's death. In an important sense, the democratic transition came on the wings both of rewriting and of forgetting. The myriad avenues and boulevards that had been named after Franco himself or his prominent subordinates following the fascists' victory in 1939 were renamed. But instead of replacing them with the names of Republican heroes and martyrs—Juan Negrín, Francisco Largo Caballero, General José

Miaja—the Spanish leaders chose to use names from the royal past: the street in Madrid named after Gonzalo Queipo de Llano, one of Franco's most important generals and, briefly, his rival, became Calle del Principe de Vergara, and so on. It was a practice that was later institutionalized in the Law of Historical Memory passed by the Spanish parliament in 2007. And in a sense, even that law could reasonably be construed as being one of "historical forgetting" because, save for a few exceptions, it ordered the authorities to remove monuments, plaques, and street names that, in the words of the statute, "exalted the Civil War or the repression under the dictatorship" between 1936 and 1975.

The justification for the Pacto del olvido was similar to the one advanced in Chile when it was decided not to prosecute General Pinochet when he relinquished power: it was meant to placate Franco's loyalists, of whom there were many, including, crucially, a number inside the armed forces, at a time when the right's willingness even to acquiesce to the transition was anything but assured—a reality that the attempted coup in 1981, more than six years after Franco's death, led by a Guardia Civil colonel, Antonio Tejero, demonstrated all too painfully. From the start, the pact had many detractors, not just on the left. And even a substantial number of those who did not oppose it in principle thought that it would not succeed unless accompanied by a South African– or Argentine-style Truth Commission. But as has so often been the case where human rights are concerned, it eventually fell to a magistrate to try to initiate through judicial procedures what the politicians continued to steadfastly refuse to contemplate. In 2008, Judge Baltasar Garzón, the same magistrate who had issued the arrest warrant for Pinochet, opened an investigation into the deaths of the 114,000 people estimated to have been murdered by the fascist side both during the Civil War itself and in the subsequent decades of Franco's rule. Garzón also demanded that nineteen mass gravesites be opened and the bodies exhumed.

Garzón's efforts were immensely controversial in Spain, not only because many Spaniards were still convinced that the Pacto del olvido had worked, but also because the country's 1977 Amnesty Law holds that murders and atrocities committed by either side during the Civil War that could be categorized as having had what the statute calls "political intention" were sheltered from prosecution. Garzón denied that he had exceeded his authority. "Any amnesty law," he argued, "that seeks to whitewash a crime against humanity is invalid in law." His many supporters in Spain, the most ardent of whom belonged to the Association for the Recovery of Historical Memory, agreed and did a great deal to sway Spanish public opinion in favor of what he was trying to do. And even though, in the end, higher courts not only overruled Garzón but went on to suspend him from the judiciary (in 2014 he became one of the lead attorneys representing the founder of Wikileaks, Julian Assange), his supporters have never wavered in their conviction that Garzón's actions represented the only ethically licit response. This was summed up by the rhetorical question that has appeared intermittently on the Association's website: "Why have the authors of the Constitution left my uncle in a ditch?"

Garzón's views are strikingly similar to those of Elie Wiesel, who believes that finding out the truth about what happened to the victims of Franco is both a moral and a legal obligation, binding for society as a whole, no matter what backroom deals politicians may have made in the 1970s. The general tendency among human rights activists, including members of the judiciary such as Garzón, has been to present law and morality as inseparable, at least in cases when the matter under consideration is clearly within the jurisdiction of a court. And because most of them assume that justice is the essential prerequisite for lasting peace, they tend to downplay when they don't categorically dismiss the risk of any negative political and social consequences flowing from their actions. But in the event that such consequences do occur, their stance has generally been that it is the politicians' responsibility, and not theirs, to sort them out.

It would be dishonest to focus on whether there might be times when remembrance could be thought of as either not yet being helpful (to peace, to reconciliation) or, alternatively, as having outlived its usefulness, without acknowledging the many instances in which forgetting, too, may have a lifespan, and at times quite a short one. This is a point that the Association for the Recovery of Historical Memory made repeatedly in its campaign in support of what Garzón was trying to do. From an analytical point of view, furthermore, the group made a valid point when it argued that "the Amnesty law was key to moving from an atrocious dictatorship to democracy, and for years benefitted from wide popular support. But in this decade [the 2000s], the victims turned to a government of the Left so that there will no longer be impunity for the crimes against humanity [committed during the Civil War and under the Franco dictatorship]."

The Association was also probably right when it claimed that twenty-first-century Spain no longer needs the Pacto del olvido, just as when *The Sorrow and the Pity* finally aired on French television it soon became clear that France had changed sufficiently that the truth about what had happened during the Occupation caused no grievous harm to the country's moral or historical ecology. But in both France and Spain, for all the difficulties they face—including terrorism and, in France's case, the continued expeditionary campaigns in the Sahel related to it—the major wars and great crimes are almost certainly behind them.[4] What this means is that the risks that come with remembrance are probably manageable, even if the rewards may not prove to be as great as the activists, international lawyers, and human rights campaigners both in NGOs and in the universities routinely claim. This is not where the dangers of remembrance lie; except for terrorists—which in France and Spain nowadays almost invariably means jihadis—no one in either country is likely to kill or to die because of what has been forgotten or failed to have been forgotten, or what has been remembered or has failed to be remembered. In many parts of the world, however, killing and dying are exactly the stakes, and it is with regard to those places that the issue of whether we should stop praising remembrance and start praising forgetting is most acute.

The places to which this has applied in the very recent past or applies now are glaringly obvious: the Balkans, Israel-Palestine (and much of the rest of the Islamic Middle East), Ireland. In other places, it is less a question of "forgetfulness now" as of the realization that at some point in the future, whether that moment comes relatively quickly or is deferred for a long time, the victories, defeats, wounds, and grudges being commemorated would be better let go. That list would include, for starters, Sri Lanka, Colombia, Ukraine. And at or at least near the top, it would also include the United States and the memory of the attacks of September 11, 2001.

4. To be clear, this claim is comparative, not an assertion that these states are not now committing crimes or will not do so in the future.

EIGHT

Against Remembrance

On September 11, 2011, the tenth anniversary of the attacks that destroyed the Twin Towers of the World Trade Center in Lower Manhattan, the official memorial was dedicated at Ground Zero. Designed by the architect Michael Arad and the landscape architect Peter Walker and titled "Reflecting Absence," the memorial is a little under eight acres in size and consists of two sunken reflecting pools, each surrounded by an enormous waterfall, the largest humanmade waterfalls in North America. The names of the 2,983 people who died on September 11, 2001, and in the failed 1993 attempt to destroy the towers are etched on the bronze panels edging the memorial pools. The closing sentence of the memorial's mission statement reads, "May the lives remembered, the deeds recognized, and the spirit reawakened be eternal beacons, which reaffirm respect for life, strengthen our resolve to preserve freedom, and inspire an end to hatred, ignorance, and intolerance."

These are unexceptional sentiments. A memorial is a place for solidarity rather than subtlety, deference rather than criticism, piety rather than revisionism. But in affirming that remembrance is humanly necessary, we must not pretend that it is ever completely innocent, not even when, in Todorov's sense (and not allowing for this, in my view, is one of the most serious limitations to his argument), it does not seem to involve any abuse of memory and when its promises to offer an exemplary lesson for both the present and the future seem credible. In the case of the 9/11 memorial, its mission statement poses more questions than it answers. For although there is nothing morally problematic about remembering the fallen and honoring the heroism of the first responders, the call to "strengthen our resolve to preserve freedom" is anything but an innocent piety. To the contrary, it bears echoes of President George W. Bush's speech to a joint session of Congress nine days after the attacks in which he argued that they had occurred because the terrorists "hate our freedoms—freedom of religion, our freedom of speech, our freedom to vote and assemble and disagree with each other."

Even those who have accepted Bush's account, despite its failure to acknowledge the possibility that it was America's actions globally rather than the American way of life that the jihadis hated, presumably would grant that the president was making a political claim in the broad sense. That the opening of the memorial marked an event that is seared into the lives and consciousness of most Americans should not obscure the fact that the ghost at the banquet of all public commemorations is always politics, whether for the Renanist purpose of mobilizing national solidarity and what might be called memorial unity, as the ceremonies at the 9/11 memorial were clearly meant to do, or for the purpose of serving as a vehicle for undermining the version of history a state propagates, one that, through the creation of some form of what is sometimes called countermemory, initiates, then speeds up, and finally helps institutionalize whatever social transformations a particular activist group has been campaigning for.

In the specific case of 9/11, it is important not to exaggerate. Whatever meaning historians eventually assign to the attacks (assuming a consensus is ever arrived at, which hardly can be taken as a given), it is highly unlikely that commemorations of them will harm America as a society, even if Americans are unlikely to learn much from them either, any more than one does from eulogies at a funeral. In an important sense, for a great many of the relatives and friends of those who died on that day, remembrance has afforded a measure of recognition and consolation, if not of closure—one of the more malign and corrosive psychological fantasies of the age. Commemorations are not generally valued for their ability to shed light on the truth. And that is entirely appropriate.[1] The problem is that such piety both nourishes illusions about how long human beings can remember, and, far more seriously, puts considerations of the grave political consequences it can engender out of bounds. And yet, in light of the dismal fact that there have been many occasions in the past when remembrance has been the incubator of a determination of a defeated people or group to secure vengeance, no matter how long it takes or what the human cost of doing so will be—think of Ireland, Bosnia, Kosovo—such deference to collective grief and trauma, not just humanly understandable but honorable as it generally is, can cost nations and societies dearly, at a price that may be exacted for generations.

---

1. The Latin phrase *De mortuis nil nisi bonum,* "Of the dead speak only the good," has often been lampooned with the quip *De mortuis nil nisi bunkum,* but this is wrong. Candor during a commemoration is not admirable but rather childish and self-serving.

Commemorations of national tragedies such as the September 11 attacks are also occasions for the affirmation of the wholly illogical belief that events that quite rightly seem central to us today will be as or almost as important to our descendants long after those of us who lived through them are dust. This assumption is not only almost certainly false; it also carries risk, especially for rich societies such as those of the United States, Canada, and the nations of the European Union. In these countries, there is a growing tendency to conflate desire with fate, wish with reality, and most relevantly in terms of collective memory, commemoration, and group remembrance, the present with eternity. Among the other effects of this is a reluctance to acknowledge and draw the difficult lessons from not just individual human transience but societal, national, and civilizational transience as well. For hopes and desires almost invariably have been poor guides where history is concerned. To insist on this is not to say that on the tenth anniversary of the attacks, those who participated should have forsworn such illusions, however indefensible they are intellectually. In that specific case the alternative would have been to state that sooner or later our descendants will forget about them, and that would have been as unbearable as it was both cruel and pointless.

What is open to question is not whether, as Kipling and Shelley knew, the most monumental accomplishments and deepest sorrows of human beings will be forgotten over the long run, but rather where the temporal outer limits of a society's capacity for remembrance, commemoration, celebration, and mourning are. In June 1940, as he tried to rally his people for what he called the Battle of Britain, Winston Churchill said, "If the British Empire and its Commonwealth last for a thousand years, men will still say, 'This was their finest hour.'" What is remarkable about his speech in terms of collective memory is that even at his most floridly rhetorical, Churchill, one of the most intransigent defenders of the British Empire ever to have lived, was nonetheless a good enough student of history neither to imagine nor to suggest that his country's imperium could last more than a millennium. If anything, that *If* at the beginning of his sentence seemed to suggest that he thought that its reign would be considerably shorter. And lest it be forgotten, even Adolf Hitler spoke of a "thousand-year Reich," not of an eternal one.

In the American context, compare the use of the memory of Pearl Harbor, first by Franklin D. Roosevelt in the immediate aftermath of the Japanese attack on the U.S. fleet in Hawaii, and then by George W. Bush in the wake of 9/11, and consider the difference between what people in FDR's time and people sixty years later expected to be remembered. FDR referred to December 7, 1941, the day the attack took place, as "a date which will live in infamy." Worth noting is that even in this formulation, Roosevelt sensibly did not say that the date would live in infamy for a thousand years, let alone *forever*. He knew better than that; he was speaking for his listeners in the here and now.

There is little doubt that on December 7, 1951, ten years after Pearl Harbor, the date continued to live in infamy for most Americans, just as 9/11 does in 2015, as I write. But the history of the memory of Pearl Harbor offers instruction in how transient the vivid remembrance of even fairly recent historical traumas can be. Anyone with half a heart and no countervailing political agenda or allegiance who goes to the Pearl Harbor memorial today will almost certainly be immensely moved, perhaps even to anger as well as grief. But how many twenty-first-century Americans still remember the 1,177 American sailors killed on the U.S.S. *Arizona* that day, most of whose remains lie directly under the memorial? And before long, those who lived through the attack, or were old enough at the time to know it had occurred, will have died. At that point, Leon Wieseltier's point about the U.S. National Holocaust Museum— that before long visitors would come when the *living* memory of Shoah had disappeared—will apply to the Pearl Harbor memorial as well.

And what about FDR's prediction that the Japanese attack would "live in infamy"? During the 1950s many Americans refused to buy German cars, while anger at the Japanese remained palpable. It is tempting to argue that reconciliation with Germany took place because the Germans themselves acknowledged their guilt and, in important ways, created a state whose essence was the antithesis of Nazi Germany. But a similar process of reconciliation followed by forgetting took place vis-à-vis Japan, even though there was no German-style contrition there. Indeed, the extent to which the Japanese persist in refusing to acknowledge the crimes they committed between the start of the Second Sino-Japanese War in 1937 and Japan's surrender in 1945 remains a profound source of anger to China and Korea, whose people were the principal victims. Yet almost no one in the United States thinks angry thoughts about the Japanese every December 7 (or on any other day of the year for that matter). And the scenario of an American refusing to contribute to a fund to help the survivors of the tsunami that struck Japan in 2011 on the grounds of what the Japanese had done at Pearl Harbor is ludicrous. Yet it would have been anything but ridiculous on December 7, 1951. To the contrary, in analogous circumstances then, such a rancorous response would not have surprised anyone.

The Second World War is over, not only in reality but also in people's hearts, just as all wars must end, including those that seem interminable, as is the case of the so-called Long War against the jihadis of the early twenty-first century. This truth can only offer cold comfort while a conflict rages on, however, and that is where the risks that remembrance will prolong a war come in. Will remembrance have this effect in the case of the commemorations of 9/11? It is too early to say. In 2015, fourteen years after the attacks on the towers, and with even the "end of the beginning" of the Long War, to use the words Churchill applied to the British victory over the Germans at El Alamein in 1942, not even in sight, there can be no question of either forgetting or forgiveness. But if it is far too early to move toward either, surely it is anything but premature to ask whether peace will ever come without our society being open to both. For even the work of mourning, essential as it is, must eventually end if life is to go on. The South African writer Nadine Gordimer once remarked that she believed writers should write as if they were already dead. On a certain level, asking people to forgo remembrance, and possibly even embrace forgetting, is also to ask them to behave as if they were already dead. We are back to Miłosz's adage about there being no other memory but the memory of wounds.

Perhaps these memories are too precious for human beings to give up. For societies, especially societies and groups that either feel themselves to be under existential threat or want to impose their own religion, or values, or territorial demands on their neighbors, the possibility may be still more remote, particularly if the collective memories, however dubious historically, seem to fuel these efforts. Consider, for example, the use Daesh, al-Qaeda, and other jihadi groups, and, for that matter, many mainstream Islamic clerics, from Indonesia to the suburbs of Paris, have made of the words "Crusade" and "Crusader." As the Cambridge social historian Paul Connerton, arguably Halbwachs's most gifted inheritor, has pointed out, "Medieval Muslim historians did not share with the medieval European Christians the sense of witnessing a great struggle between Islam and Christendom for control of the Holy Land." Connerton added that the words "Crusade" and "Crusader" never appear in the Muslim chronicles and other historical writing of the time; instead they use the terms "Franks" or "infidels." But according to Connerton, beginning sometime in the nineteenth century "an expanding body of Arabic historical writing has taken the Crusades as its theme," with the term becoming "a code word for the malign intentions of the Western powers . . . culminating in the foundation of the State of Israel." On Connerton's reading, at least, one of the effects of each of the Arab-Israeli wars has been to galvanize further studies of the Crusades.

The Crusaders as proto-Zionists! It may not be history, but it offers a textbook case of the development and then of the deployment of political collective memory in the service of large-scale solidarity—yet another iteration of those "griefs requiring common efforts" that Renan advanced as the sine qua non of nation-building. The fact that virtually nothing in the contemporaneous Arab writing about the Crusades supports the Arab world's collective memory of those griefs is neither here nor there. That the myth fills a need, and subsequently can be manufactured convincingly enough to captivate and inspire those to whom it is directed, is what matters. Think of it as the transformation of the wound into the weapon.

The renowned British historian of the Crusades Jonathan Riley-Smith believes that the construction of what remains the consensus collective memory in the Muslim world of the Crusades began in the late nineteenth century when Sultan Abdulhamid II described the European imperial powers' conquests

of Ottoman lands as a new crusade. In 1915 it seemed appropriate to name the new university in Jerusalem after Saladin, who,
as Riley-Smith puts it, began to be praised by Arab nationalist
writers for having undone the first European seizure of the Holy
Land when, at the Battle of Hattin in 1187, he put an end to the
nearly century-old Christian Kingdom of Jerusalem that had
been established in the aftermath of the First Crusade in 1099.
By the 1980s, this association between the Kingdom of Jerusalem
and the modern State of Israel had come to seem so self-evident
to many Arab artists and intellectuals that the Palestinian poet
Mahmoud Darwish could write of the Israeli siege of Beirut in
1982 as being the work of "leftover Crusaders . . . taking their
revenge for all medieval history."

Less than two months after the September 11 attacks,
Osama bin Laden recorded a speech in which he described the
U.S. invasion of Afghanistan that was only then just beginning
as linked to "a long series of crusader wars against the Islamic
world." These had not only happened in the immediate post–
World War I period in which, as he described it, "the whole
Islamic world fell under the crusader banner—under the
British, French, and Italian governments." For bin Laden, these
efforts at conquest had taken place without respite throughout
the twentieth century and included Russia's wars in Chechnya
and the actions of "the crusader Australian forces [who landed]
on Indonesian shores . . . to separate East Timor, which is part
of the Islamic world."

The late twentieth and early twenty-first centuries in the
Islamic world have been a graveyard of many forms of rationality, but most notably of skepticism. And in the context of piety
and ressentiment now running rampant in the ummah, it seems
inconceivable that at least a large number, though of course not
all, of those who watched bin Laden's speech on social media

or, for that matter, read Darwish's words, found themselves "remembering" this crusader "past," in which Balian of Ibelin (c. 1143–1193), the great Christian knight of the Kingdom of Jerusalem; John III Sobieski (1629–1696), the Polish king who lifted the Ottoman siege of Vienna in 1683; Ferdinand de Lesseps (1805–1894), the French developer of the Suez Canal; Field Marshal Edward Allenby (1861–1936), the British commander whose army captured Jerusalem from the Ottomans in 1917; David Ben-Gurion (1886–1973), the main founder of the State of Israel; Boris Yeltsin (1931–2007), the president of the Russian Federation during the first Chechen War; and John Howard (born 1939), the Australian prime minister who ordered Australia's intervention in East Timor in 1999, all fuse together to become leaders of the same now millennium-old crusade to subjugate the Islamic world.

That this is a manipulation of history of the grossest kind and is in fact an *anti*-historical exercise of the contemporary political imagination should be obvious. But that bin Laden's understanding is accepted as history throughout the Islamic world should be equally clear. Tzevtan Todorov would be within his intellectual rights to insist that the bin Laden view exemplifies the abuse of collective memory. And yet a principal element of his argument, one that in some ways is the key to his claim to distinguish between remembrance's proper use and its abuse, would be easy to adopt for someone wanting to make the case for the truth of bin Laden's account. Recall how Todorov distinguished between what he called "literal" memory and "exemplary" memory, in which the former, "particularly when pushed to extremes, carr[ies] [great] risks," while the latter, "potentially liberating," offers an exemplum from which "one draws a lesson [and in which the past offers a principle of action for the present]."

Surely an advocate of bin Laden's viewpoint would insist that this is exactly what al-Qaeda's leader was doing when, to use part of Todorov's description of what exemplary memory can achieve, he took instances from the past "as a model for understanding new situations, with different participants," thus opening a particular memory "to analogy and generalization." For wasn't this why bin Laden annexed the contemporary assault (as he saw it) to the Crusades and generalized from that analogy? And when Todorov writes that one of the attributes of exemplary memory is to make it possible to "make use of the lessons of [past] injustices to combat those that are occurring today, to leave the self and go toward the other," could not a bin Laden supporter legitimately claim that this was precisely his goal as well and muster as evidence for this the incontrovertible fact that the Western colonial powers did dominate the Islamic world for centuries—a domination that to a considerable extent the American empire, informal though it is, has tried to maintain?

Todorov knows this, and, immediately after laying out the distinction between the literal and the exemplary, he is quick to emphasize that "self-evidently not all lessons are good ones." But his idea that we will be able to distinguish good ones from bad ones through "universal rational criteria" hardly provides the prophylactic against the "bad lesson" that he seems to think or at least hope they do. Human beings are not as rational as this argument supposes. More important, *pace* John Gray, incommensurability is often a more reliable guide than universality to the realities of our world. It is also vital to fully take on board the degree to which, as Wieseltier has put it, "memory has become our mysticism, so great that it is the generation of authenticity that it confers. It would be too strong to call it a hoax, but it is certainly a kind of trick." And therein lies the problem.

Wieseltier is right to add that "the effect [of the trick] evaporates in the sunlight of critical history." But critical anything has always been and always will be a minority taste, while the appetite for the mystical and the authentic is as voracious as it is universal, which is what Karl Kraus was getting at when he contrasted Beethoven to the hurdy-gurdy and the memory. This is the unpalatable truth that even minds as fine and deep as Todorov's and Margalit's don't seem able to accept about collective memory when they offer their nuanced and admirably contingent claims for what, at its best and in many contexts, it undoubtedly can achieve. For when in history has the mystical *ever* played second fiddle to the critical?

It certainly is not common in political systems, or, for that matter, within social movements of any kind, and becomes ever less likely the more extreme such systems are. The political theorist Karl Deutsch once quipped (the remark is sometimes wrongly attributed to Renan), "A nation is a group of people united by a mistaken view of the past and a hatred of their neighbors." He was exaggerating. But it is no exaggeration to say that collective memory is the ideal delivery system for such mistaken views. The fact that in most of the rich world state-centric, top-down, triumphalist collective memory has ceded a great deal of ground to the claims of what Jeffrey Olick has called "the politics of regret" does not change this. To the contrary, Renan's idea that what bound a nation together was the "spiritual principle" has proved to work equally well for groups demanding recognition and redress in this age of destabilized national identities. The odds are stacked in favor of the mystical, and it makes no more sense to bet against this than it does for a gambler to bet against the house in a casino.

Wieseltier once warned that nationalist politics grounded in collective memory can "destroy the empirical attitude that is necessary for the responsible use of power." It is an insight that events in the Middle East, that proving ground for the *irresponsible* use of power, seem to confirm every day. To take only one of myriad examples, when Israeli forces encircled Beirut in 1982, Israel's then prime minister, Menachem Begin, announced that the Israeli Defense Forces had the "Nazis surrounded in their bunker," even though it was Yasser Arafat and Fatah that were trapped in the Lebanese capital. It was a paradigmatic example of what happens when collective memory born of trauma finds political and, above all, military expression. Margalit may be correct to insist that this need not be the result of collective memory, but even he concedes that collective memory is *usually* manipulated. If this is the case, surely what collective memory brings about—and not only in Israel-Palestine—is more important than what it might accomplish in an ideal situation.

Israel offers a florid illustration of how disastrously collective memory can deform a society. The settler movement routinely appeals to a version of biblical history that is as great a distortion of that history as the Islamist fantasy about the supposed continuities between the medieval Kingdom of Jerusalem and the modern State of Israel. At the entrance to the settler outpost of Givat Assaf on the West Bank, a placard reads, "We have come back home." In an interview, Benny Gal, one of the settlement's leaders, insisted, "On this exact spot, 3,800 years ago, the land of Israel was promised to the Hebrew people." Shani Simkovitz, the head of Gush Etzion, the settlement movement's principal "philanthropy," echoed Gal's claim: "More than three thousand years ago our fathers gave us a land, which is not Rome, it is not New York, but this: the Jewish land."

Even when it is secular, mainstream Zionist collective memory is often as mystical and as much of a manipulation of

history as these views. Consider the simultaneous mythologiz-
ing and politicization of archaeology in Israel that has now
reached the point where scholarship and state-building have
come to seem like two sides of the same coin. Writing in 1981,
Amos Elon observed that Israeli archaeologists were "not
merely digging for knowledge and objects, but for the reassur-
ance of roots, which they find in the ancient Israelite remains
scattered throughout the country." He added, "The student of
nationalism and archaeology will be tempted to take note of
the apparent cathartic effects of both disciplines."

Nowhere has this been more evident than in the use of
the ruins of the fortress of Masada, which were excavated in the
early 1960s by Yigael Yadin, the retired IDF chief-of-staff turned
archaeologist. It was at Masada that the Jewish Zealots who had
risen in revolt against Roman rule in the year 70 of the Common
Era made their last stand and where they eventually committed
mass suicide (the story is chronicled by Flavius Josephus in *The
Jewish War*). Soon after Yadin's excavations had been com-
pleted, fledgling soldiers in the Israeli military's armored corps
began to be brought to the site for their passing-out parades.
There, along with the standard ceremonies that accompany the
end of basic training in any army, the graduates would chant,
"Masada will never fall again." As Elon pointed out, such "historical" evocations, which he called ceremonies "staged by
secular moderns over the graves of ancient religious zealots,"
were in reality completely ahistorical. "The zealots of Masada,"
he wrote, "would no doubt have opposed modern Israel's West-
ernized and secular character just as they opposed the Roman-
ized Jews of their time."

Elon was thinking within the framework of critical history. He is skeptical of group memory, above all because he
knows it to be unreliable. In contrast, Yigael Yadin, who in one

of his last interviews spoke approvingly of what he called Israel's "Masada Complex," can be legitimately interpreted as having devoted his archaeological career to restoring what the critic Harold Bloom, in his foreword to Yerushalmi's *Zakhor*, called "the lost coherence of Jewish memory at its strongest, which was messianic and therefore redemptive." Here is Yadin in Masada in 1963, addressing an IDF armored corps graduation ceremony: "When Napoleon stood among his troops next to the pyramids of Egypt, he declared: 'Four thousand years of history look down upon you.' But what would he not have given to be able to say to his men: 'Four thousand years of your own history look down upon you.'"

Four thousand years of history. How can Wieseltier's empirical attitude, necessary for the responsible exercise of power, compete with that? Let us not pretend that such exhortations are not better for group cohesion than Elon's critique and, more generally, his ambivalence. For if history teaches us anything, it is that in politics as in war, human beings are not hard-wired for ambivalence; they respond to loyalty and certainty. And just as Renan had argued in "What Is a Nation," to the extent these can be strengthened by collective remembrance, it is of no importance whether the memories in question are historically accurate or if, instead, they are inventions of purely modern manufacture.

Only one important twentieth-century European thinker, the German political philosopher Ulrich Beck, has directly confronted this problem. In a number of his works, Beck suggested that it might be possible to replace the "national grandeur" template for collective memory, which he called "methodological nationalism," with some form of national "shared ambivalence" about the past, though he is less clear than he might be on how this would work in practice. France is a good example, for it remains the "capital" of the memory industry, the avant-garde of what Pierre Nora has dubbed a "universally guilty conscience." Presumably Beck would have supported a school syllabus that would be attentive to both the Enlightenment and the slave trade, the French Revolution and the Algerian War. But he never explained how studying history in all its ambivalence, which, as Nora has warned, runs the risk of leading to a whole-sale criminalization of France's past, would be a better guide for young French people than focusing on the triumphant na-tional mythmaking of the past as their predecessors did until at least the early 1970s. No, there is no going back, but the multi-culturalist mirror image of the older pedagogy does not seem to be working very well either.

Yosef Yerushalmi thought that the fundamental problem with the modern age was that without some form of command-ing authority, which he thought of in terms of what in the Jew-ish tradition is called *halakhah,* and what less parochially might be thought of as moral law, people no longer knew what need-ed to be remembered and what could safely be forgotten. But however moving, Yerushalmi's veneration of memory as the guarantor of tradition, and his horror at the possibility that in the modern era this chain of tradition is in the process of being broken on the wheel of forgetfulness, calls out to a moral struc-ture under sentence of death. For despite the talk of the central-ity of identity politics to modern self-understanding, the kind of fixed identity that Yerushalmi deemed essential for the suc-cessful transmission of a community's traditions through the generations has become ever more difficult to maintain. Instead, in Marx's grand phrase, "All that's solid melts into air."

But if Yerushalmi's fears were warranted, and any real continuity between past, present, and future has been broken, replaced by collective memories of the past that are no more real than the invented traditions whose study Hobsbawm and Ranger pioneered, then surely the time has come to scrutinize our inherited pieties about both remembrance and forgetting. A good place to start might be the Edict of Nantes, issued by Henri IV in 1598 to bring to an end to the wars of religion in France. Henri quite simply forbade all his subjects, Catholic and Protestant alike, to remember. "The memory of all things that took place on one side or the other from March 1585 [forward] . . . ," the edict decreed, "and in all of the preceding troubles, will remain extinguished, and treated as something that did not take place." Would it have worked? Could such bitterness really have been annealed by royal fiat? Since Henri was assassinated in 1610 by a Catholic fanatic opposed to the edict, which itself was eventually repealed, we can never know. But is it not conceivable that were our societies to expend even a fraction of the energy on forgetting that they now do on remembering, and if it were accepted that in certain political circumstances at least the moral imperative might be Nietzsche's "active forgetting," not Santayana's "those who forget the past are condemned to repeat it," peace in some of the worst places in the world might actually be a step closer?

As a reporter during the Bosnian War, which was in large measure a slaughter fueled by collective memory, or, more precisely, by the inability to forget, I used to carry with me increasingly creased and faded copies of two poems by the Polish poet Wisława Szymborska. In both "The End and the Beginning" and "Reality Demands," that most humane and antidogmatic of poets, a woman who once said that her favorite phrase had become "I don't know," certainly understood the moral imperative of forgetting. She had lived through Poland's agonies under Germans and Russians alike. For her, as for the majority of her generation, the soil of her nation's countryside and the paving stones of its cities were drenched in blood, suffused with memories of the most tragic, unbearable, and destructive character. And yet, Szymborska concluded "The End and the Beginning" with these words:

> Those who knew
> what was going on here
> must make way
> for those who know little.
> And less than little.
> And finally as little as nothing.
>
> In the grass that has overgrown
> causes and effects,
> someone must be stretched out
> blades of grass in his mouth
> gazing at the clouds.

In "Reality Demands" she went farther:

> Reality demands
> we also state the following:
> life goes on.
> It does so near Cannae and Borodino,
> At Kosovo Polje and Guernica.

What Szymborska articulates in both poems is the ethical imperative of forgetting so that life can go on—as it must. And she is right to do so. For everything must end, including the work of mourning and with it Miłosz's memory of wounds. Otherwise the blood never dries, the end of a great love becomes the end of love itself, and, as they used to say in Ireland, long after the quarrel has stopped making any sense, the memory of the grudge endures. Those who insist on the centrality of forgiveness are right up to a point. But forgiving is not enough because it can never escape its own contingency. "I do not speak either of vengeance or of forgiveness," Borges wrote. "Forgetting is the only vengeance and the only forgiveness." Perhaps he went too far. But without at least the option of forgetting, we would be wounded monsters, unforgiving and unforgiven ... and, assuming that we have been paying attention, inconsolable.